Quiet Strength

Navigating Teenage Years for Introverts

Jennifer Costanza

MA, LMFT

Table of Contents

Introduction

You're back in high school, a place buzzing with energy, a hub of endless activity and noise. But amid this whirlwind, there you are, moving through the corridors like a quiet observer in a loud, vibrant world. You're the one who doesn't jump into conversations spontaneously or vie for the spotlight in class discussions. Instead, you find comfort in the background, observing, thinking, and understanding the world from your vantage point.

Let me draw you a more vivid picture. It's lunchtime, and the cafeteria is alive with the disharmony of chatter and laughter. You pick a spot at the edge of the room, a small table that becomes your island in the sea of noise. While others are busy exchanging stories, you're lost in your thoughts, maybe pondering over a book you read last night or a project you're passionate about. You're not antisocial; you're just wired differently. You prefer meaningful conversations with a close friend to small talk with a crowd.

Now, think about those group projects. You're in a team, but your ideas often stay locked inside your head. It's not that they aren't good; in fact, they're often innovative and well-thought-out. But the loud voices seem to drown yours out before they even leave your lips. You wonder, *Is there something wrong with me?* You watch as the extroverts shine, their energy seemingly unbounded, and you question your place in this high-energy setting.

But here's where the story takes a turn. One day, you're assigned a project on a topic you love. For the first time, you feel a surge of excitement, an eagerness to dive in. You start working on it, and suddenly, you're in your element. The ideas flow effortlessly, and when you present them to your group, there's a noticeable shift. They listen, genuinely interested, as you speak with a confidence that surprises even you. In that moment, you realize your quiet nature is not a barrier but a bridge to deep, thoughtful insights.

Remember the school parties? The ones where the music blared so loud it felt like it was shaking your core? You were there but not fully present. You'd stand by the wall, sipping a drink, watching the sea of dancing bodies, feeling out of sync with the rhythm of the room. You'd wonder what it would be like to let go, to be in the center of the dance floor, laughing and moving without a care in the world. But that wasn't you, and that's perfectly okay. Your rhythm was different, but it was there, steady and sure, in your quiet observation of the world around you.

In all these moments, what stands out is not the silence of your voice but the depth of your inner world. A world rich with thoughts, ideas, and dreams that don't always need the loudness of words to be valid or valuable. Your journey through high school as an introvert wasn't about fitting into a mold; it was about understanding and embracing your unique way of experiencing the world. But what if I told you that your quiet nature, your introspective soul, is not just a part of you but a strength? What if the very traits you thought were your weaknesses are, in fact, your superpowers in this loud, chaotic world? This is the heart of our journey together in this book.

Remember the times when you felt out of place at those high-energy parties or when group projects felt more draining than collaborative? We've all been there. It's like being a left-handed person in a world designed for the right-handed—everything feels a bit off. But here's the twist: Being left-handed (or, in our case, being an introvert) isn't a disadvantage; it's a different kind of advantage.

Now, let's embark on a journey of self-discovery, where we delve deep into the world of introverts. Let's delve into the intricacies of different personality types, dispel common misconceptions about introverts, and discover how being an introvert in high school is not merely about enduring but flourishing in a manner that is distinctively yours.

We will dissect the stereotypes and reveal how introverts, extroverts, and even ambiverts—those wonderful blends of both—interact, complement each other, and sometimes even overlap. Did you know that introverts can be just as socially adept as extroverts, but perhaps in smaller, more meaningful gatherings? Or that an introvert's need for solitude is not a sign of social anxiety but a way to recharge and reflect?

Our journey will take us through the complexities of personality fluidity, the art of blocking out noise without shutting out the world, and the exquisite pleasure of immersing oneself in flow states—those moments where time stands still, and you're completely absorbed in an activity you love.

We'll balance the scales between personal crafts and social hobbies, showing you how to navigate both worlds without losing your essence. And most importantly, we'll talk about defining yourself on your terms—not as the world wants you to be, but as who you truly are.

Chapter 1:

Am I Different?

Let's imagine a scenario. You're at a bustling party, the music's pulsing, laughter, and chatter filling the air. Yet, there you are, in the midst of it all, feeling like a square peg in a round hole. You watch extroverts effortlessly glide through the crowd, charming and energetic, and you can't help but wonder, *Am I different?* This feeling, my friend, isn't just you. It's a shared experience among many, often leaving us questioning our place in a world that seems to celebrate the loud and the bold. But what if I told you that being an introvert, or somewhere in between, isn't just okay? It's a superpower in disguise.

In this chapter, we will unravel the mystique of introverts, extroverts, and the fascinating blends in between known as ambiverts. We'll explore the unique qualities that set introverts apart from their extroverted counterparts and how these differences are not just mere personality traits but are deeply rooted in our psychological makeup.

Introverts vs extroverts: What makes them different? We'll dive into the science behind the brain's wiring that dictates whether you're more likely to recharge in solitude or thrive in the company of others. We'll examine how these variances appear in daily life, including in how we make decisions and interact socially. Recognizing and understanding these differences can pave the way for enhanced self-awareness and personal development.

Introverts and extroverts: What makes them similar, and what attributes of an introvert work well with those of an extrovert? Beyond the differences, there's a beautiful synergy between introverts and extroverts. We'll explore the yin and yang of these personality types, uncovering how their attributes can complement each other in relationships, work environments, and beyond. It's about appreciating the strengths of these differences and finding a harmonious balance.

Then, there are the ambiverts who embody the fluidity of both introversion and extroversion. We'll delve into how ambiverts adapt to different situations, influenced by their emotional states and environments. Understanding this blend can be particularly insightful for those who resonate with both ends of the spectrum.

By the end of this chapter, you'll have a deeper appreciation for the qualities that make you, and those around you, uniquely introverted, extroverted, or ambiverted. It's about embracing these qualities and harnessing them to work in your favor in a world that often feels like it's made for one type of person. Whether you're the life of the party or the one enjoying it from the sidelines, remember: your personality is your unique imprint on the world, and it's worth celebrating.

Introverts vs. Extroverts: What Makes Them Different?

Diving into the worlds of introverts and extroverts is akin to exploring two distinct landscapes, each with its unique terrain and climate. At their core, these personality types differ primarily in how they recharge, engage with the world, and process information. The distinction, however, is more nuanced than a simple binary. It's a spectrum where energy dynamics and social preferences play pivotal roles.

Energy Source and Recharge

The most striking difference lies in their energy source. Introverts are akin to a contemplative walk in a serene forest—they draw power from solitude and quiet environments. Like recharging batteries in a peaceful nook, they need alone time after social engagements. Conversely, extroverts are like a vibrant street festival—they gain energy from the buzz of people and activity. They thrive in lively settings and often seek the word of a crowd to recharge their spirits (Leonardo, 2019).

Social Preferences

This energy dynamic directly influences their social preferences. Introverts often opt for deep, meaningful conversations and smaller, intimate gatherings akin to a cozy coffee shop chat. Extroverts, however, are comfortable in larger, more dynamic social settings—reminiscent of a bustling marketplace, where interactions are plentiful and varied.

Processing Information

When it comes to processing information, introverts and extroverts differ significantly. Introverts often reflect deeply, processing their thoughts internally before expressing them—like a painter carefully planning their strokes. Extroverts, conversely, process their thoughts through engagement and dialogue, akin to a jazz musician improvising in the moment.

Comfort With Solitude vs. Social Situations

Introverts find solace in solitude; too much socializing can leave them feeling drained. Extroverts, in contrast, may find prolonged solitude disquieting, craving social interaction to re-energize.

Introverts and Extroverts: Similarities and Complementary Attributes

Despite these differences, introverts and extroverts share several commonalities and possess attributes that can beautifully complement each other.

Seeking Meaningful Human Connections

Both introverts and extroverts share a fundamental human desire for meaningful connections. They may approach relationships differently, but the end goal of forming genuine bonds is a common thread that weaves through their interactions.

Adaptability in Various Situations

Both personality types exhibit a remarkable ability to adapt to different social scenarios. Introverts can sometimes step into an extroverted role, showcasing surprising sociability in certain contexts like leadership or public speaking. Extroverts, too, can embrace moments of introspection and solitude, finding value in quieter, reflective activities.

Ability to Balance Each Other

In relationships, the attributes of introverts and extroverts can create a harmonious balance. An extrovert's ease in navigating social settings can help an introvert feel more at ease in group interactions. Conversely, an introvert's propensity for deep listening and thoughtful conversation can encourage an extrovert to explore more reflective and introspective sides.

Bringing Diverse Strengths to the Table

In team environments or group projects, the distinct strengths of introverts and extroverts can synergize to create a dynamic and effective unit. Extroverts might lead the charge in energizing the group and fostering team spirit, while introverts contribute careful planning and insightful analysis.

Embracing the Fluidity of Ambiversion

The concept of ambiversion illustrates that many people exhibit both introverted and extroverted traits, depending on the context. This fluidity suggests that personality traits are not rigidly defined but exist on a spectrum, allowing for a more dynamic interplay of characteristics.

Opportunities for Mutual Learning and Growth

Both introverts and extroverts can learn valuable lessons from each other. Introverts can adopt some of the extrovert's spontaneity and ease in social situations, while extroverts can learn the art of introspection and the value of solitude from introverts.

In essence, while introverts and extroverts navigate the world differently, they share the fundamental human need for connection and have much to offer each other. When embraced and understood, their differences can lead to enriching relationships and mutual growth. The dance between these two personality types, when in sync, creates a dynamic and balanced rhythm in the tapestry of human interaction.

The Ambivert's Social Dynamics

In a world often seen in black-and-white terms of introversion and extroversion, ambiverts emerge as a fascinating blend, embodying the strengths of both. They navigate social and solitary waters with a finesse that's both enviable and intriguing.

The Spectrum of Social Engagement

Ambiverts possess a remarkable social fluidity. In a group setting, they can engage, initiate conversations, and actively participate in discussions. However, unlike extroverts, they don't always seek the spotlight. They're equally content listening and observing. This adaptability is their forte, allowing them to fit into various social scenarios effortlessly.

Energy Management

For ambiverts, energy management is akin to walking a tightrope between social interaction and solitude. They need to balance these aspects to maintain their emotional well-being. After an evening in a bustling social setting, an ambivert might find solace in a day spent in quiet reflection or pursuing a solitary hobby, effectively recharging their batteries.

Empathetic and Balanced Communication

Ambiverts are often skilled communicators. They harness the introspection of an introvert with the outward focus of an extrovert. This duality makes them excellent at understanding different perspectives. In conversations, they can oscillate between being an attentive listener and a vibrant speaker, making them relatable and effective in personal and professional interactions.

The Challenges for Ambiverts

Being an ambivert offers unique benefits, yet it also presents specific challenges that can be confusing for the ambiverts and those in their social circle.

Navigating the Misunderstanding

The fluid nature of an ambivert's personality can sometimes lead to misconceptions. One day, they might be mistaken for an extrovert, while on another day, their introverted side is more prominent. This shifting can be puzzling for others, leading to misunderstandings about their true nature.

Struggling With Internal Balance

The ambivert's need to strike a balance between introversion and extroversion can sometimes be a tough act. Leaning too much toward one end of the spectrum can lead to feelings of exhaustion or isolation. It's a delicate equilibrium that requires constant self-awareness and adjustment.

Tips for Ambiverts

Navigating the world as an ambivert can be smoother with a few mindful strategies.

Cultivating Self-Awareness

Recognizing your current need for social interaction or solitude is key. This self-awareness helps in making decisions that align with your emotional and mental state, ensuring you don't overextend yourself socially or isolate too much.

Open Communication

Explaining your ambivert nature to friends, family, and colleagues can help them understand your varying social needs. It's okay to articulate when you need a break from social activities or when you're craving more interaction.

Leveraging Your Flexibility

Ambiverts should view their adaptability as a strength, not a liability. This unique trait allows them to thrive in diverse situations—from leading a team project to enjoying a solitary hike. Embracing this versatility can lead to personal growth and fulfillment.

Mindful Balancing of Social and Solitary Time

Keeping an eye on your energy levels and mood can guide you in balancing your time between socializing and solitude. Listening to these internal cues is essential for maintaining emotional and mental well-being.

In a nutshell, ambiverts hold a special place in the spectrum of personalities. They bring a unique set of skills and challenges to the table.

Understanding and embracing these aspects can lead to a fulfilling and balanced life, both socially and personally.

In Essence

In the vivid tapestry of human personalities, introverts, extroverts, and dynamic ambiverts create a rich mosaic of characteristics and tendencies. As we've journeyed through the nuanced landscapes of these personality types, we've seen that each holds its unique superpower. Introverts, with their deep wells of introspection, and extroverts, with their vibrant energy, both contribute significantly to the richness of human interactions. Ambiverts, balancing on the spectrum's fulcrum, bring a blend of empathy, adaptability, and balanced communication, making them relatable and effective in various settings. Yet, with these strengths come challenges, particularly for ambiverts, who must navigate the fluidity of their personality and the misunderstandings it can sometimes breed. The key, as we've discovered, is self-awareness, open communication, and leveraging the flexibility that defines them. In embracing and understanding these diverse personality traits, we find not only a greater appreciation for ourselves but also for those around us, fostering a world where every personality, whether introverted, extroverted, or somewhere in between, is celebrated for its unique contribution to the symphony of human experience.

Chapter 2:

Introversion at Its Core

Picture yourself navigating the bustling hallways of high school, where every corner echoes with laughter, chatter, and the constant buzz of social activity. Now, imagine feeling like an observer in this lively world, preferring the serene company of your thoughts or a small, trusted group of friends. This describes the universe of an introvert—a domain characterized by profound contemplation, vibrant imagination, and a heightened sense of self-awareness. Far from the misconception of social anxiety, introversion is a unique landscape of the mind that shapes how one interacts with the world and builds networks, even in environments that seem overwhelmingly extroverted.

In this exploration, we delve into the essence of introversion, unraveling its fundamental traits and distinguishing it from social anxiety. The journey begins with an understanding of the roots of an introvert, appreciating the intrinsic qualities that define this personality type. It's a misconception that introverts are plagued by social anxiety; instead, they exhibit a preference for solitude or the presence of a few close companions. Their world is rich with imagination, preferring reflection and conceptual thought over immediate action. This chapter aims to demystify introverts, revealing how their high levels of self-awareness contribute to a unique perspective in social settings. Introverts are not socially anxious by default; their enjoyment of social interactions is often balanced with a need for solitude to recharge. Understanding this delicate balance is key to appreciating the introverted experience, especially in contexts like the high school social scene, where their social batteries might differ significantly from their more extroverted peers.

The Roots of Introversion

Introversion fundamentally revolves around energy dynamics in social situations. Introverts expend energy in these settings. They need solitude to recharge and thrive (Cherry, 2013). This preference for alone time is often misinterpreted. It's not a dislike for people or social interactions; rather, it's about the way introverts process their experiences and regain their energy.

Key traits of introverts include a tendency toward deep reflection and a preference for quiet, less stimulating environments. They often enjoy solitude, not out of fear or anxiety, but because it provides a space for introspection and rejuvenation. Introverts are typically thoughtful and deliberate in their actions and decisions and may take time to open up to others. They often have a small, close-knit circle of friends, valuing deep, meaningful connections over broader social networks.

Importantly, introversion is not synonymous with social anxiety. Social anxiety is a mental health condition characterized by intense fear and discomfort in social situations, often accompanied by a fear of being judged or embarrassed (National Institute of Mental Health, 2022). While an introvert may choose solitude over a social gathering, a person with social anxiety might avoid social situations due to fear, even if they desire social interaction.

Introverts and Socialization

Introverts, by their very nature, often prefer their own company or the presence of a small, select group of individuals. This preference is deeply rooted in their personality traits and how they experience and process the world around them.

Firstly, introverts find solace and rejuvenation in solitude. Unlike extroverts, who gain energy from social interactions, introverts recharge by spending time alone. This time is not just a retreat from the noise of the world; it's a valuable period for introspection, reflection, and engaging in activities that they find fulfilling and intellectually stimulating, such as reading, writing, or pursuing creative hobbies.

When introverts do choose to socialize, they typically prefer small gatherings or one-on-one interactions. Large groups or crowded social settings can feel overwhelming and draining for them. In smaller settings, introverts are able to engage more deeply and meaningfully. They value quality over quantity in their social interactions, seeking genuine connections rather than superficial exchanges. This preference for depth in relationships is often reflected in how they choose their friends; introverts tend to have a smaller circle of close, trusted friends rather than a wide network of acquaintances.

It's important to note that preferring solitude or small groups doesn't mean introverts are antisocial or lack social skills. On the contrary, they can be very sociable and enjoy meaningful conversations. However, their socialization is often more intentional and selective, focused on connections that they find genuinely rewarding.

Furthermore, introverts often possess a rich inner life filled with a vivid imagination and deep thoughts. They tend to be contemplative, reflective, and self-aware. This inward orientation means they are often content in their own company, exploring their thoughts and ideas without the need for constant external stimulation.

Self-Awareness in Introverts

When we talk about self-awareness in introverts, we're delving into a nuanced and multifaceted aspect of their personality. Self-awareness, at its core, is the conscious knowledge of one's own character, feelings, motives, and desires. For introverts, this self-awareness is often a natural extension of their personality traits.

The introspective nature of introverts plays a critical role in fostering self-awareness. They tend to spend a significant amount of time in self-reflection, quietly analyzing their thoughts and feelings. This introspection isn't a sporadic exercise for them; it's an integral part of their daily lives. Whether they're pondering over past interactions, contemplating future decisions, or assessing their emotional state, introverts are constantly engaged in a process of self-evaluation and understanding.

This tendency for introspection is amplified by their preference for solitude. In their quiet moments, introverts are not just seeking respite from the external world; they are actively engaging with their inner selves. This engagement allows them to develop a deeper understanding of their motivations and desires. The quietude provides a backdrop for a rich inner dialogue, where introverts can process their experiences and emotions without external interference. Moreover, introverts often possess a keen sense of observation, not just about the world around them but also about their internal processes. They are typically more aware of subtle shifts in their mood and thought patterns. This heightened internal sensitivity is a significant factor in their ability to understand and regulate their emotions effectively.

Additionally, introverts' approach to social interactions also contributes to their self-awareness. While they might be quieter in groups, they are often observant and thoughtful listeners. This ability to listen and observe not only makes them attuned to others but also helps them reflect on their own reactions and feelings in social settings. However, it's important to acknowledge that self-awareness is a spectrum, and not all introverts may exhibit the same level of self-awareness. Various factors, including life experiences and personal growth efforts, can influence an individual's level of self-awareness.

In essence, self-awareness in introverts is a complex interplay of their introspective nature, preference for solitude, observational skills, and thoughtful approach to social interactions. These aspects combine to create a rich internal landscape where introverts can explore and understand the depths of their personality.

Introverts and Social Anxiety

Introverts, by nature, tend to derive their energy from within. They enjoy social interactions but in moderation. Their need for alone time is not driven by fear or anxiety but by a preference for introspection and solitude. This alone time is essential for them to recharge and reflect, which in turn allows them to appreciate and engage in social interactions more fully when they do occur. The key here is balance—introverts balance their social engagements with periods of solitude to maintain their mental and emotional well-being.

Social anxiety, on the other hand, is characterized by a persistent fear of social situations. Individuals with social anxiety may dread and avoid social interactions due to fears of judgment, embarrassment, or scrutiny. It's important to note that social anxiety can affect anyone, regardless of whether they are introverted or extroverted. When socially anxious individuals do engage in social situations, they might indeed exhibit a greater "social battery" than many introverts. This is because their avoidance of social situations is not a preference but a coping mechanism for their anxiety. Once they are in a social setting and overcome the initial barrier of fear, they might find themselves participating more actively, sometimes even more than typical introverts.

It's essential to understand these distinctions to avoid misconceptions about both introverts and those with social anxiety. While introverts choose solitude out of preference, socially anxious individuals often find themselves compelled to avoid social interactions out of fear. Recognizing and respecting these differences can lead to greater understanding and support for individuals who experience these traits.

Introverts and Mental Health

Introverts, with their unique inward-focused nature, face distinctive challenges and possess particular strengths when it comes to mental health. Understanding these nuances is crucial for introverts themselves and for those around them.

Handling mental health for introverts requires a nuanced approach, one that respects their intrinsic need for solitude while acknowledging the importance of connection and self-awareness. As individuals who often find strength and rejuvenation in quiet reflection, introverts face unique challenges in maintaining mental wellness. Their natural tendency toward deep introspection, sensitivity to their environment, and preference for meaningful social interactions can significantly influence their mental health. Thus, it is crucial for introverts to adopt strategies tailored to their specific personality traits, ensuring a harmonious balance between their inner world and external demands.

Balancing Solitude and Social Interaction

Strategic Solitude

Introverts need to identify the right amount of alone time that rejuvenates without leading to isolation. This might involve setting aside dedicated periods for solitude amidst a busy schedule.

Quality Over Quantity in Socializing

When engaging socially, introverts should prioritize meaningful interactions. This could mean choosing small gatherings or one-on-one meetings over large, noisy events.

Intentional Scheduling

Planning social activities in a way that allows for subsequent downtime can help introverts recharge and prevent burnout.

Mindful Introspection

Techniques like meditation can help introverts observe their thoughts without getting overwhelmed, allowing for a healthier internal dialogue.

Journaling

Writing down thoughts and feelings can provide an outlet for introspection, helping to process emotions in a constructive manner.

Cognitive Reflection

Regularly assessing one's thoughts and feelings can help in recognizing patterns, such as tendencies toward negative thinking, and addressing them proactively.

Self-Compassion and Acceptance

Recognizing the strengths of being an introvert and accepting this trait can boost self-esteem and reduce feelings of being "out of place."

Combating Self-Criticism

Developing affirmations or engaging in positive self-talk can counteract tendencies toward self-criticism.

Seeking Inspirational Stories

Learning about successful introverts can provide motivation and a sense of belonging.

Managing Sensitivity

Introverts need to establish boundaries to protect their energy, such as limiting time in overly stimulating environments.

Relaxation Techniques

Practices like deep breathing, yoga, or spending time in nature can help introverts manage their sensitivity to external stimuli (Shapperd, 2023).

Expressive Arts

Creative outlets like painting, music, or writing can be therapeutic for introverts, providing a way to process and express emotions.

Seeking Quality Connections

Building a few close, trusted relationships can provide the emotional depth and understanding introverts crave.

Community Involvement

Engaging in community activities or groups based on shared interests can offer social interaction that feels meaningful and less draining.

Online Communities

For introverts who find in-person interactions challenging, online forums or groups can be a valuable source of connection.

Professional Help When Needed

Being aware of signs of mental distress and acknowledging when professional help is needed is crucial for introverts.

Finding the Right Therapist

Introverts should look for therapists who understand their introverted nature and can provide tailored support.

Exploring Different Therapy Modalities

Different approaches, like cognitive-behavioral therapy or art therapy, can be explored to find what resonates best with an introvert's personality.

The Importance of the Environment

The environment plays a significant role in how introverts experience and manage their mental health. A supportive, understanding environment that respects their need for alone time and deep connections can significantly enhance their ability to cope with mental health challenges.

The Role of Self-Awareness

Self-awareness is a powerful tool for introverts. Understanding their own patterns, triggers, and needs enables them to take proactive steps in managing their mental health, from setting boundaries to engaging in activities that foster well-being.

In essence, while introverts may face unique challenges in managing their mental health, they also possess distinct strengths. By leveraging these strengths, understanding their needs, and seeking support when necessary, introverts can navigate their mental health with confidence and resilience.

In Essence

In the vibrant realm of human personality, introverts often navigate a unique path, especially in environments teeming with extroverted energy. This exploration has illuminated the distinctive ways introverts experience and process the world around them, highlighting the crucial differences between introversion and social anxiety. At the core, introverts are characterized by their preference for solitude and deep, meaningful connections, thriving in environments that resonate with their introspective nature. Far from being hindered by social anxiety, they simply operate on a different frequency, finding rejuvenation in quiet moments and smaller, intimate gatherings. With a profound level of self-awareness, introverts possess the ability to navigate social landscapes with a thoughtful, reflective approach, cherishing quality interactions over quantity. As we conclude this journey into the heart of introversion, it becomes evident that understanding and embracing these traits is key to fostering mental wellness and harmony in a world that often celebrates the louder, more visible aspects of social interaction.

Chapter 3:

Personality Types

Imagine you're at your school reunion, surrounded by former classmates, each showcasing a distinct blend of traits and quirks. There's the ever-charismatic Emily, effortlessly weaving through the crowd, leaving a trail of laughter in her wake. In stark contrast, there's Michael, absorbed in a deep, thoughtful conversation in a quieter corner. These diverse personalities, vibrant and complex, are the essence of what makes human interactions fascinating and unpredictable. But have you ever wondered what lies beneath these surface-level characteristics? What if I told you that the key to understanding yourself and others goes far deeper than the generic labels of "introvert" and "extrovert"?

This exploration delves into the intricate world of personality types, unraveling the psychology that shapes our interactions and self-perception. The journey begins with a comprehensive view of the psychological foundations of personality, exploring the "Big Five" personality traits and their significance in our lives. We delve into the nuances of these traits, examining how they shape our decisions, relationships, and even career paths.

From there, we enter the fascinating realm of personality subsets, illuminated by renowned frameworks like the Myers-Briggs Type Indicator. These detailed classifications offer a more granular view of our individuality, revealing the subtle interplay between different aspects of our personality. By understanding these dimensions, you'll gain insights into why you think and act the way you do and how you can leverage these traits to your advantage.

We'll also explore how personality types are not just theoretical concepts but have practical applications in various settings, from corporate environments to educational institutions. The intriguing parallels between personality types in the workplace and those found in a high school setting will be drawn, providing a unique perspective on how these traits manifest at different stages of life.

As we delve deeper, the "Big Five"—openness to experience, conscientiousness, extraversion, agreeableness, and neuroticism— become sharper focus. Each trait holds the key to unlocking a more profound understanding of human behavior and personality dynamics (Cherry, 2023a).

The Psychology of Personality Types

The concept of personality is a captivating and intricate subject that delves into what makes each individual unique. At its core, personality encompasses the diverse array of enduring traits and characteristics that shape our thoughts, emotions, and behaviors. It's a blend of patterns deeply ingrained within us that influences how we interact with the world and perceive our place within it. Personality is not just a static set of traits but a dynamic and evolving aspect of our being, influenced by both inherent dispositions and the multitude of experiences that we encounter throughout life.

When exploring personality through a psychological lens, a particularly illuminating framework is the Big Five personality traits model. This model, grounded in decades of psychological research, distills personality into five fundamental dimensions. Each of these dimensions exists on a continuum, with every individual exhibiting varying degrees of each trait. Understanding these traits not only offers insights into our own behaviors and motivations but also enhances our comprehension of others, fostering empathy and effective communication.

Openness to Experience

This trait is marked by a curiosity about the world and a receptiveness to new experiences, ideas, and values. Individuals high in openness tend to be imaginative, creative, and open-minded (Johns, 2023). They are more likely to embrace novel ideas, enjoy diverse cultural experiences, and engage in unconventional thinking. On the other hand, those lower in openness might prefer routine, have more conventional interests, and be more resistant to change. Openness shapes how we engage with new ideas and experiences, influencing our creativity and willingness to venture beyond our comfort zones.

Conscientiousness

This dimension reflects the degree of organization, dependability, and discipline an individual exhibits. Highly conscientious people are generally meticulous, responsible, and reliable. They tend to plan ahead, follow through with commitments, and exhibit a strong sense of duty. Lower levels of conscientiousness might manifest as a more relaxed or spontaneous approach to life, possibly leading to disorganization or procrastination. Conscientiousness impacts our ability to set and achieve goals, maintain order, and fulfill obligations.

Extraversion

Extraversion is characterized by sociability, energy, and an outward orientation toward the social world. Extroverted individuals typically enjoy being around people, are energetic, and often seek stimulation in the company of others. They tend to be talkative, assertive, and enthusiastic. Conversely, introverts (those lower in extraversion) might prefer solitude, require less social stimulation, and often find deep fulfillment in introspective activities. Extraversion influences how we derive energy and satisfaction from our social interactions and environments.

Agreeableness

This trait reflects the extent of a person's altruism, trust, and cooperative spirit. Highly agreeable individuals are often compassionate, friendly, and eager to help others. They value harmony, are often trusting, and strive to avoid conflict. Those lower in agreeableness may be more competitive, skeptical, and less inclined to compromise. Agreeableness shapes our interactions with others, affecting our capacity for empathy, cooperation, and the maintenance of social harmony.

Neuroticism

Neuroticism refers to the tendency to experience negative emotions like anxiety, sadness, and anger. Individuals high in neuroticism may be more prone to emotional instability and react more intensely to stressors (Widiger & Oltmanns, 2017). They might struggle with mood fluctuations and find it challenging to cope with stress. On the flip side, those with lower levels of neuroticism are generally more emotionally resilient and less likely to be upset by stressful situations. Neuroticism affects our emotional well-being and how we cope with the challenges and stressors of life.

In understanding these dimensions, it's crucial to remember that no single trait exists in isolation. Our personalities are shaped by the unique interplay of these traits in combination with our life experiences and environmental factors. The Big Five model not only provides a framework for self-reflection and personal growth but also offers valuable insights for improving interpersonal relationships and fostering a deeper understanding of human behavior. It's a testament to the rich complexity and diversity of human personality, highlighting the multifaceted nature of what it means to be uniquely ourselves.

Various Personality Types

Personality psychology offers an intriguing and diverse array of theories and frameworks. Among them, the Myers-Briggs Type Indicator (MBTI) emerges as one of the most prominent and extensively acknowledged instruments (Cherry, 2023b). This model delves into the intricate nuances of human behavior and thought processes, categorizing individuals into 16 distinct personality types based on four primary dichotomies: Extraversion (E) vs. Introversion (I), Sensing (S) vs. Intuition (N), Thinking (T) vs. Feeling (F), and Judging (J) vs. Perceiving (P). Among these, INTP, INFJ, and ENFP represent three uniquely intriguing personality types, each with its own set of characteristics, strengths, and challenges (Simkus, 2022).

INTP (The Architect or Thinker)

- **Overview:** INTPs are known for their love of logic and a relentless drive toward understanding. They are often seen as the architects of ideas and theories.

- **Key traits:** INTPs are highly analytical, often diving deep into subjects they find intriguing. They are abstract thinkers, often lost in thought, contemplating various possibilities. These individuals are independent, original, and creative, with a unique perspective on life.

- **Studies and relevance:** Research suggests that INTPs thrive in environments that allow them to explore concepts and theories. They excel in fields like science, technology, and philosophy. The analytical prowess of INTPs makes them excellent problem-solvers, though they may struggle with practical and routine tasks.

INFJ (The Advocate or Counselor)

- **Overview:** INFJs are known for their idealism and moral compass. They are often seen as counselors or advocates, driven to help others and make the world a better place.

- **Key traits:** INFJs are insightful, compassionate, and highly intuitive. They are deeply committed to their values and often have a clear vision of how to improve the lives of others. They can be reserved, but they form deep connections with people.

- **Studies and relevance:** Studies indicate that INFJs are drawn to careers that align with their values and offer a sense of purpose. This includes roles in education, counseling, and the arts. INFJs 'empathetic nature equips them well for roles that involve nurturing and caring for others, though they may become overwhelmed in highly chaotic or conflict-driven environments.

ENFP (The Champion or Inspirer)

- **Overview:** ENFPs are effervescent and charismatic, often seen as inspirers and motivators.

- **Key traits:** ENFPs are highly imaginative and creative and exude a contagious enthusiasm for life. They are excellent communicators, adept at inspiring and motivating others. They value meaningful connections and are often spontaneous and flexible.

- **Studies and relevance:** Research has shown that ENFPs gravitate toward careers that allow them to express their creativity and connect with others, such as marketing, journalism, and the performing arts. Their adaptability and people skills make them excellent team players, though they may struggle with highly structured or repetitive tasks.

Myers-Briggs Type Indicator

- **Background:** The MBTI, developed by Isabel Briggs Myers and her mother, Katharine Cook Briggs, is rooted in Carl Jung's theory of psychological types. It was designed to make Jung's theory understandable and useful in people's lives (The Myers-Briggs Company, 2009).

- **Scale and relevance:** The MBTI categorizes people into 16 personality types based on their preferences in four areas. It has been a valuable tool in personal development, career planning, team building, and improving interpersonal relationships. The MBTI helps individuals understand their own and others' behaviors, thereby fostering better communication and understanding in various aspects of life.

Understanding personality types like INTP, INFJ, and ENFP through the lens of the MBTI offers invaluable insights into human behavior and preferences. These insights can be harnessed in personal development, career choices, and improving interpersonal dynamics. While the MBTI and its personality types are not without criticism, particularly regarding their scientific rigor, their widespread use and the depth of understanding they provide into human nature make them an essential tool in the realm of personality psychology.

MBTI and High School

In the fascinating world of personality typologies, various frameworks offer insights into human behavior and preferences, notably in organizational contexts. Translating these frameworks to a high school setting can provide educators and administrators with valuable tools for understanding and nurturing student development. Let's delve into some prominent type indicators and then explore how the four personality types commonly used in organizations can be adapted to high school environments.

Myers-Briggs Type Indicator (MBTI)

The MBTI, based on Carl Jung's theory of psychological types, categorizes personalities into 16 types, derived from four dichotomies: Introversion/Extraversion, Sensing/Intuition, Thinking/Feeling, and Judging/Perceiving. Each type represents a unique combination of these preferences, influencing how individuals perceive the world and make decisions (Cherry, 2023c).

INTJ (Introversion, Intuition, Thinking, Judging)

Often known as the "Architect," INTJs are strategic and logical and enjoy complex problem-solving. They are contrasted with the ESFP (Extraverted, Sensing, Feeling, Perceiving), known as the "Performer," who are sociable, spontaneous, and focused on the here and now.

ENFP (Extraverted, Intuition, Feeling, Perceiving)

Characterized as an enthusiastic innovator, adept at exploring new possibilities and ideas. They differ significantly from ISTJs (Introverted, Sensing, Thinking, Judging), who are practical, orderly, and value tradition and consistency.

The Big Five Personality Traits

As we have learned, the Big Five Personality Traits model, a renowned psychological framework, offers a comprehensive lens to understand human personality. Unlike typological models that categorize individuals into distinct types, the Big Five assesses personality across five broad spectrums: Openness, Conscientiousness, Extraversion, Agreeableness, and Neuroticism (OCEAN) (Ackerman, 2017). When applied to a high school setting, this model transforms into a powerful tool, enabling educators to tailor their teaching methods, foster a supportive learning environment, and guide students in their personal and academic development. Understanding these traits in the context of young learners can profoundly influence how educators approach teaching, counseling, and student engagement, ultimately contributing to a more nuanced and effective educational experience.

Openness

Students high in openness are often curious, imaginative, and open to new experiences. In a high school environment, these students might thrive in creative subjects like arts and literature and may benefit from an interdisciplinary approach to learning. Conversely, students who are lower in openness could prefer structured, fact-based learning environments, excelling in areas like mathematics and science.

Conscientiousness

Highly conscientious students tend to be organized, reliable, and hardworking. Teachers can support these students by providing clear guidelines and structured goals. Students with lower conscientiousness might benefit from more engaging, interactive teaching styles to help them stay focused and motivated.

Extraversion vs. Introversion

Extraverted students usually enjoy group work and active class participation, while introverted students might prefer individual assignments or working in smaller groups. Recognizing these traits can help teachers balance classroom activities to cater to both types of students, ensuring that each has an environment conducive to their personal comfort and learning style.

Agreeableness

Students with high agreeableness typically have strong cooperative skills and may excel in team-based projects or leadership roles in group settings. For those with lower agreeableness, activities that challenge them to work in teams or partnerships can be beneficial for developing empathy and collaboration skills.

Neuroticism

This trait pertains to emotional stability. Students with high levels of neuroticism may experience stress and anxiety more frequently, affecting their academic performance and social interactions. Schools can provide resources like counseling services, stress management workshops, and a supportive environment that acknowledges and addresses these challenges.

Understanding a student's personality profile can be incredibly valuable in guiding them toward potential career paths. For example, students high in openness and extraversion might be well-suited for careers in communication, arts, or public relations, while those who score high in conscientiousness and low in neuroticism might excel in careers requiring detail orientation and steadiness, like accounting or engineering.

Similarly, extracurricular activities can be tailored to cater to different personality traits. For instance, debate clubs may attract extroverted students, while creative writing or science clubs might appeal to introverted students. Sports and team-based activities can be excellent for students with high agreeableness, promoting teamwork and cooperation. By understanding the diverse personality traits of students, educators can foster a culture of inclusivity and respect. This understanding can also guide anti-bullying campaigns and conflict resolution strategies, ensuring a safe and welcoming environment for all students.

In Essence

As we gather at a school reunion, surrounded by a spectrum of former classmates like the charismatic Emily and the contemplative Michael, we are vividly reminded of the rich diversity of human personalities. Our exploration into the intricate world of personality types, guided by the "Big Five" traits and the Myers-Briggs Type Indicator, has not only illuminated the complex psychology that shapes our interactions and self-perception but also revealed the fascinating parallels in a high school setting. This journey has underscored the importance of understanding these personality frameworks, not just as theoretical concepts but as practical tools in education and personal development. It's a profound reminder of how our unique blends of traits and quirks, so evident in the microcosm of a school reunion, weave the fabric of our individual and collective experiences, shaping our paths from the classrooms of our youth to the diverse walks of life we tread today.

Chapter 4:

The Fluidity of Personality Types

Imagine a world where your personality, like water, adapts and molds itself to the environment you find yourself in. Picture yourself at school, laughing and joking around with your friends, your personality shining bright and carefree. Fast forward a few hours, and you're at a family gathering, your demeanor shifts to being more respectful and attentive. This everyday magic—the way your personality seems to shape-shift depending on where you are and who you're with—is at the heart of this chapter.

This chapter delves into the intriguing idea that while the core of who we are remains constant, our personalities are not rigid structures but rather dynamic and adaptive elements of our being. The key takeaway here is profound yet simple: While the fundamentals of what makes you a person are unwavering, personality types can often change to adapt to a given situation, as many of the personality types share a lot of commonalities.

The fluidity of personality is a double-edged sword. It can make you an unwavering force in situations demanding resilience or a pushover in environments where assertiveness is key. Understanding and harnessing this fluidity, therefore, becomes crucial. This chapter will guide you through the nuances of this concept, shedding light on how a healthy understanding of when to access certain traits in your personality can be more valuable than the fluidity itself.

Understanding Personality Fluidity

Personality fluidity, a term capturing the dynamic nature of an individual's characteristic patterns of thought, emotion, and behavior, is an intriguing concept in the realm of psychological development. Rather than being fixed and immutable, personality traits can evolve over time, influenced by a variety of factors, including life experiences, social interactions, and internal psychological processes (Zaman & Jameel, 2021).

The Concept

At its core, personality fluidity suggests that our traits are not set in stone. This concept aligns with the notion that individuals are capable of change and adaptation throughout their lives. It's a departure from the traditional view of personality as a static, unchanging entity, embracing the idea that while certain core aspects of our personality may remain stable, other facets can shift in response to life's demands and experiences.

Various elements contribute to this fluidity. Environmental factors, such as cultural norms, social settings, and personal relationships, play a pivotal role. Internal factors, including emotional maturity, cognitive development, and personal experiences, also significantly impact personality development and change.

Personality Fluidity as a Double-Edged Sword

The concept of personality fluidity, the ever-evolving mosaic of our characteristic thoughts, emotions, and behaviors, stands as a testament to the human capacity for change and adaptability. However, it's akin to walking a tightrope; on one side lies the realm of resilience and adaptiveness, and on the other, the risk of losing one's core identity. This double-edged sword, intrinsic to the human psyche, plays a pivotal role in our interactions with the world and our inner selves.

Adaptability and Growth

The positive aspect of personality fluidity is seen in its promotion of adaptability. In an ever-changing world, the ability to adjust one's behavior and attitudes is invaluable. This adaptability can manifest as increased resilience in the face of adversity, an openness to new experiences, and the flexibility to adopt different perspectives. It encourages personal growth, fosters the development of a wide range of coping strategies, and can lead to increased empathy and understanding of others.

Consistency and Core Identity

While adaptability is advantageous, maintaining a consistent core identity is equally important. A well-defined sense of self provides stability and direction. It acts as a compass, guiding decisions and actions that align with one's values and beliefs. This consistency is crucial for forming and maintaining healthy relationships and for setting boundaries that protect one's mental and emotional well-being.

Vulnerability to External Influences

The downside of personality fluidity becomes apparent when individuals lack a firm foundation in their identity. In such cases, they may become overly susceptible to external influences, from peer pressure to societal norms, which can lead to a chameleon-like existence. This vulnerability can manifest in diminished self-esteem, increased anxiety about social acceptance, and a tendency to compromise one's values and beliefs to fit in.

Prevalence of Personality Fluidity in Teens

Adolescence is a critical juncture in the development of personality fluidity. This period, marked by a search for identity and a heightened sensitivity to external influences, sees teenagers navigating a complex landscape of self-discovery and social conformity. The prevalence of personality fluidity in this stage of life not only shapes immediate experiences but also lays the groundwork for future personality development.

Exploration and Identity Formation

During adolescence, individuals experiment with different roles, behaviors, and identities. This exploration is a natural part of their quest to establish a unique self-identity. Teenagers are often influenced by their peers, media, and other external factors as they try on different personas, which can lead to significant changes in their behavior and attitudes.

Impact of Social Dynamics

The social environment plays a crucial role in shaping a teenager's personality. Peer groups, family dynamics, and societal expectations can either support or hinder the development of a stable and authentic self-identity. Teens are particularly susceptible to peer pressure, and the desire for acceptance can lead them to adopt behaviors and attitudes that may not align with their true selves.

Risks to Mental Health

The fluid nature of personality in adolescence, while a natural part of development, can pose risks to mental health. The conflict between an authentic self and an adopted persona, as indicated by the research of Soller (2014), can lead to feelings of inauthenticity, contributing to mental health issues such as anxiety, depression, and a diminished sense of self-worth (Bromley et al., 2006). It's crucial for teenagers to develop coping mechanisms and support systems that help them navigate these challenges.

Long-Term Developmental Implications

The patterns and traits developed during adolescence can have lasting effects on an individual's personality. While some traits show stability, others continue to evolve. Understanding the mechanisms and impacts of personality fluidity during this formative stage can help in guiding teens toward healthy and positive personal development, ensuring they grow into adults who are both adaptable and true to their core selves.

In essence, personality fluidity, in both its positive and negative aspects, plays a significant role in human development, particularly during the tumultuous teenage years. It's a journey of balancing adaptability with a firm sense of self, a challenge that, when navigated well, can lead to a rich, fulfilling, and authentic life.

A Healthy Understanding of Your Personality Traits

Having a healthy understanding of when to access certain traits in your personality is immensely valuable, especially for teens navigating the complexities of growing up. Let's break this down in detail.

Recognizing Your Traits

Personality traits are like tools in a toolbox. Each one has its purpose. For example, traits like conscientiousness, agreeableness, and openness can shape how you interact with the world. However, being aware of which trait to use and when is key. For instance, while conscientiousness (being responsible and organized) is great for schoolwork, agreeableness (being cooperative and empathetic) is better suited for teamwork and social interactions.

Fluidity vs. Stability

It's a common belief that having a fluid personality—the ability to adapt and change traits based on the situation—is beneficial. However, research suggests that personality traits have a degree of stability over time. This doesn't mean you can't change or adapt, but it highlights the importance of understanding and utilizing your stable traits effectively.

The Value of Trait Selection

Understanding the value of trait selection is akin to mastering the art of choosing the right tool for a specific task. Just as a skilled craftsman selects the appropriate tool from their toolkit, so must we learn to select the right personality traits for different situations. This process is more than mere adaptability; it's about strategically leveraging our inherent qualities to achieve the best outcomes in our personal, academic, and professional lives. By doing so, we align our actions with our goals, ensuring a more harmonious and effective interaction with the world around us.

Strategic Use of Traits

Recognizing when to exhibit assertiveness, empathy, or resilience can significantly impact the outcomes of our interactions. For example, assertiveness might be crucial in a debate, while empathy is key in comforting a friend.

Balancing Traits

It's about finding a balance between different traits. Being too assertive can be perceived as aggressive, while being overly empathetic might lead to neglecting one's own needs.

Self-Improvement

Conscious trait selection can be a pathway to personal growth. It encourages self-reflection and a deeper understanding of one's strengths and areas for improvement.

Application in Real-Life Scenarios

Applying the concept of trait selection in real-life scenarios is what brings this knowledge to life. Whether it's navigating the complexities of interpersonal relationships, tackling academic challenges, or advancing in our careers, the ability to appropriately harness our personality traits can be a game-changer. This application requires not just self-awareness but also an acute understanding of the context and the needs of the situation at hand.

Interpersonal Relationships

Knowing when to be empathetic, when to draw boundaries, and when to be assertive can deepen relationships and prevent misunderstandings.

Academic and Professional Success

Traits like conscientiousness and openness to experience are invaluable in academic settings, while leadership and assertiveness can propel one's career forward.

Adapting to Change

Life is full of unexpected changes and challenges. Traits like flexibility and resilience become essential in adapting to new environments or overcoming obstacles.

Challenges for Teens

For teens, the journey of understanding and applying trait selection is uniquely challenging. Adolescence is a critical time for personality development, marked by exploration, identity formation, and increased social dynamics. Teens face the daunting task of navigating these complexities while trying to remain authentic to themselves, often under the watchful eyes of parents, teachers, and peers.

Peer Pressure and Social Expectations

Teens often grapple with the desire to fit in versus staying true to their unique traits. Balancing societal expectations with personal authenticity is a delicate task.

Identity Formation

This stage of life is crucial for developing a sense of self. Teens must learn to understand and appreciate their innate traits while also being open to growth and change.

Emotional Regulation

With the myriad of emotional and physical changes happening, managing traits like emotional stability and mood swings becomes critical for mental well-being.

Future Planning

Decisions made during adolescence can have long-term implications. Understanding which traits to develop and rely on can guide teens in making informed choices about their education, career, and relationships.

Understanding when to access certain traits in your personality is not just about adapting to different situations; it's about being true to yourself while also being responsive to the world around you. For teens, this understanding is a journey—one that involves learning about yourself, experimenting with different aspects of your personality, and acknowledging that each trait has its time and place. Remember, the goal is not to change who you are but to use the best of who you are in each situation.

Fluidity Is Positive

As you grow and evolve, you'll notice something fascinating about your personality: It's fluid, adaptable, and responsive to the environments you find yourself in. This isn't just about how you change to fit into different settings; it's also about how these settings begin to respond more to your presence over time. Let's dive into this intricate dance of personality and environment.

First, it's important to grasp the concept of a fluid personality. Fluidity means you have the ability to adapt and mold yourself to different situations and social circles. This is a powerful trait, as it allows you to navigate various aspects of life with ease and grace. Whether you're with family, friends, or in a classroom, your ability to adjust your behavior, attitudes, and even your interests can be a significant asset.

The Impact of Environments on You

Different environments—like your school, home, or sports team—act as unique stages where various aspects of your personality are highlighted. For instance, in a classroom, you might be an inquisitive, studious individual, while at home, you're a caring sibling or child. Each of these settings draws out different traits and behaviors from you.

The Shift: When Environments Respond to You

As you grow older and gain more experience, a fascinating shift occurs. The environments you inhabit start responding more to your presence. This means your personality and actions begin to influence the environment itself. Let's break this down:

Growing Self-Confidence

With time, as you become more self-assured, your confidence shines through in your interactions. This confidence can positively affect those around you, making you a more influential presence in any room.

Developing a Sense of Identity

As you discover more about who you are and what you stand for, this clarity in your identity starts to impact your surroundings. You might find that you're setting trends, influencing discussions, or leading initiatives because you're more certain about your values and beliefs.

Building Relationships

The connections you forge with people around you also play a role. As you grow, these relationships mature, and your ability to influence and inspire your peers increases. Your friends, family, and even teachers begin to see and respect you for your individuality and strengths.

Learning to Influence

Your ability to affect change in your environment doesn't just happen. It's a skill you develop. You learn to communicate effectively, to empathize with others, and to stand up for what you believe in. These skills allow you to have a more significant impact on your surroundings.

Embracing the Fluidity

Embrace the fluid nature of your personality. It's not about losing yourself in an attempt to fit in; it's about understanding that you have the unique ability to adapt while maintaining your core values and beliefs. As you navigate through different stages of your life, remember:

Stay True to Yourself

While adapting to different environments is a skill, never lose sight of your core values and beliefs. Your authenticity is your strength.

Understand the Power of Influence

Recognize that as you grow, you hold the power to influence your surroundings positively. Use this power wisely and responsibly.

Keep Growing and Learning

Personal development is a lifelong journey. Keep exploring, learning, and growing. With every new experience, you add another layer to your rich personality.

Balance is Key

Find the balance between adapting to your environment and letting your environment adapt to you. It's a two-way street where both you and your surroundings grow and evolve together.

Remember, the fluidity in your personality is not just about how you change; it's also about how you influence and shape the world around you. As you continue to grow, you'll find that the rooms you are in don't just witness your presence; they respond to it, adapt to it, and sometimes, even transform because of it. This is the power of your evolving personality, a true testament to your growth and influence as a young individual.

In Essence

Concluding, the concept of personality fluidity presents a pivotal aspect of our psychological makeup. It is a dynamic, ever-changing element of who we are, adaptable and malleable in response to the diverse situations we encounter. This fluidity is both a strength and a vulnerability; it allows for resilience and adaptability, enabling us to navigate various life scenarios effectively. However, it also carries the risk of losing touch with our core identity if not harmoniously balanced with a stable sense of self. Particularly crucial during adolescence, this period of personality shaping and identity formation is marked by the delicate task of balancing adaptability with authenticity. The essence lies in understanding and selectively utilizing different personality traits as needed, not to alter our true selves but to leverage our inherent qualities in the most effective way. This is not just about adapting to fit into different settings; it's about how these settings respond to and are influenced by our presence. The fluidity in our personality is a testament to our capacity for growth, learning, and influence, a journey of finding the equilibrium between adapting to our environment and allowing our environment to adapt to us, shaping and being shaped in this intricate dance of life.

Chapter 5:

How Do I Block Out the Noise?

Imagine you're in the middle of a crucial level in your favorite video game, but your phone is buzzing non-stop, your younger sibling is blaring music, and outside, your friends are calling for you to join them. It's the typical chaos of a teenager's life, where every moment seems to bring a new distraction. This scenario might sound all too familiar to you. In a world where your attention is constantly pulled in a million directions, how do you find your focus? How do you block out the noise to concentrate on what's important to you?

The key to navigating this noisy landscape isn't about finding a silent retreat but learning the art of selective hearing and creating mental space. This chapter delves into practical, actionable strategies to help you filter out the unnecessary so you can concentrate on the essentials. It's not just about physical quietude; it's about mental clarity and emotional tranquility.

This chapter is all about mastering that skill. It's not about creating a bubble of silence; it's about learning how to tune out distractions and tune into your goals, whether it's acing that next exam, perfecting a new skateboard trick, or just finding a moment of peace to gather your thoughts.

Understanding Selective Hearing or Noise-Blocking

Have you ever been accused of having "selective hearing" by your parents or teachers? Maybe they said you're not listening, but you swear you didn't hear them. This phenomenon, often termed selective hearing or noise blocking, is quite fascinating. Let's dive into what it really is and explore how it can actually be beneficial, especially for teenagers like you. Selective hearing is like having a mental filter. Your brain decides what to listen to and what to ignore. It's not that you're purposely ignoring things (well, most of the time!); it's just how our brains are wired.

Imagine you're at a party with loud music and lots of people talking. You're trying to listen to your friend, and somehow, you can. That's selective hearing in action. Your brain is focusing on your friend's voice and filtering out the rest.

During adolescence, your brain undergoes massive changes. One of these changes affects how you process sounds. As kids, we're tuned to recognize familiar voices, like our parents. But as teenagers, our brains start to prioritize new and different voices, like those of peers or potential friends. It's nature's way of helping us become more independent and social.

Why Do Teens Have Selective Hearing?

The teenage years are a whirlwind of changes, not just physically but also mentally. One intriguing aspect of this transformation is how your hearing adjusts. Let's take a deeper look into why teens, maybe even you, experience selective hearing.

Neurobiological Changes

When you hit puberty, it's not just about getting taller or your voice changing. Your brain is evolving, too. This evolution significantly affects how you perceive and respond to sounds around you. Initially, as children, our brains are finely tuned to pick up familiar voices, especially those of our primary caregivers. This tuning is crucial for survival, ensuring that we pay attention to those who protect and nurture us. However, as you step into your teenage years, this changes. Your brain starts prioritizing unfamiliar voices. Why does this happen? It's nature's way of prepping you for adulthood. As you grow, it becomes essential to form bonds outside of your familial circle. This shift in auditory focus aids in building new social networks, which are vital for your personal and professional growth. You start to pay more attention to your friends and less to your parents, not because you're ignoring them, but because your brain is wired to do so.

Psychological Factors

Selective hearing is not just a biological response; it's also psychological. As a teenager, your mind is a bustling hub of thoughts, emotions, and interests. When you're deeply engrossed in an activity that captivates your interest—be it a hobby, a conversation, or even daydreaming— your brain puts up a sort of "Do Not Disturb" sign. It's not that you choose to ignore other stimuli, but your brain prioritizes what it finds most engaging at the moment. This focus is a natural defense mechanism against sensory overload, allowing you to concentrate on what you deem most relevant.

How Can Selective Listening Be Beneficial?

Selective listening, often misunderstood as a mere lack of attention, can actually be a powerful tool. Here's why it can be incredibly beneficial, especially for teenagers like you navigating through an ever-changing and noisy world.

In today's fast-paced world, the ability to focus amidst chaos is invaluable. Selective listening enables you to concentrate on the task at hand, even in a distracting environment. For instance, if you're studying in a noisy place, your ability to tune out irrelevant noise and focus on your study material can enhance your learning efficiency. This skill becomes increasingly important as you grow older and find yourself in environments where multitasking and focusing amidst distractions are the norms.

Social Skill Development

During your teenage years, developing social skills is crucial. Selective listening plays a vital role in this. By tuning into conversations that interest you and tuning out less relevant ones, you're able to engage more deeply with peers and build stronger relationships. This skill is not just about making friends; it's about understanding social cues, empathizing with others, and learning to navigate complex social environments. These skills are essential for personal and professional success.

Learning and Memory

Selective listening can significantly enhance your learning and memory. In a classroom setting, the ability to focus on the teacher's voice over other students' chatter allows for better comprehension and retention of the material. This focused attention leads to more effective studying, better grades, and a deeper understanding of the subject matter. It's not just about hearing the information; it's about actively listening and processing it, which is crucial for academic success.

Mental Health

Selective listening can also be a valuable tool for mental health. In an age where we're bombarded with information and stimuli, the ability to tune out negativity or stressful stimuli can be a form of self-care. For instance, ignoring hurtful comments or not getting overwhelmed by the constant stream of news can help maintain mental peace. It allows you to take control of what you consume mentally, reducing stress and anxiety.

Selective hearing isn't just about ignoring your parents when they ask you to clean your room. It's a complex brain function that plays a significant role in your development as a teenager. It helps you concentrate, socialize, and even take care of your mental well-being. So next time someone accuses you of having selective hearing, you've got some cool science to back you up! Remember, while it's a handy skill, it's also important to tune in to important stuff (like when your parents are actually calling you for dinner!). Balancing this skill with being an active listener when needed is the key to making the most out of selective hearing.

Practical Ways of Blocking Out Noise

In an environment where distractions are abundant, especially for teenagers, finding tranquility amidst chaos is not just a desire. It's a necessity for mental clarity and emotional well-being. Understanding the various ways to block out noise can significantly enhance your ability to focus, learn, and relax. Let's dive into these methods in more detail.

Earplugs

Earplugs are a simple and highly effective tool for creating silence in a noisy world. They come in different materials and designs, each serving a unique purpose.

- **Foam earplugs:** These are commonly available and affordable. They work by being compressed and inserted into the ear canal, where they expand to block out external sounds. These are ideal for studying or sleeping in a noisy environment.

- **Silicone earplugs:** These are softer and mold to the shape of your ear, providing a comfortable and custom fit. They're excellent for prolonged use, such as during a long study session or while reading.

- **High-fidelity earplugs:** These are designed to reduce noise levels evenly while maintaining sound quality. They're perfect for situations where you want to reduce volume but not completely block out sound, like during music practice or attending concerts.

When choosing earplugs, consider factors like comfort, the noise reduction rating (NRR), and the specific environment in which you'll be using them.

Creating a Quiet Space

Your surroundings play a significant role in your ability to concentrate. Creating a quiet space is more than just finding a silent room; it's about crafting an environment conducive to your mental and emotional needs.

- **Selecting the right location:** Look for a spot in your home or elsewhere that's naturally quieter. This could be a little-used room, a corner of a library, or even a peaceful outdoor setting.

- **Simple soundproofing techniques:** Minor adjustments can significantly reduce noise intrusion. Use heavy curtains to dampen street sounds, place rugs on hard floors to absorb echoes, and seal gaps under doors to keep out household noise.

- **Establishing boundaries:** Communicate with those around you about your need for quiet time. Setting clear boundaries about noise can help create a mutual understanding and respect for each other's space and needs.

Leveraging Technology

In our digital age, numerous gadgets and applications can assist in creating a quieter environment.

- **Noise-canceling headphones:** These are game-changers for studying in noisy places. They use active technology to cancel out background noise, allowing you to concentrate on your work without distractions.

- **White noise machines and apps:** These devices and apps produce soothing sounds that mask disruptive noises. They offer a range of sounds like rainfall, ocean waves, or forest ambiance, which can be calming and help improve focus.

Meditation and Mindfulness

In a world full of external noise, sometimes the loudest sounds are the ones in our own heads. Meditation and mindfulness are invaluable tools for calming internal noise.

- **Starting a meditation practice:** Begin with short, manageable sessions. Guided meditation apps specifically designed for teenagers can be a helpful starting point.

- **Mindfulness in daily activities:** Practice mindfulness by being fully present in whatever you're doing, whether it's eating, walking, or even engaging in a hobby. This practice helps train your mind to focus on the present moment, reducing stress and improving concentration.

Strategic Timing

Being strategic about when you engage in certain activities can help you make the most of quieter times.

- **Studying during off-peak hours:** Try studying early in the morning or late at night when your environment is naturally quieter. This can significantly improve your ability to concentrate and absorb information.

- **Avoiding busy places:** If you're studying in public places like libraries or cafes, try to go during less busy hours. This can help you avoid the peak times when these places are noisiest.

Embracing Nature's Quietude

Nature offers a unique brand of tranquility, often overlooked in our fast-paced, technology-driven lives. It's not just about the absence of urban noise but the presence of soothing natural sounds like rustling leaves, flowing water, or birdsong. These sounds can significantly lower stress and improve mental clarity.

Connecting With Nature

Creating an indoor green space with plants can transform your study or relaxation area into a calm oasis. Plants are natural sound absorbers, reducing ambient noise and also purifying the air.

Outdoor Activities

Engaging in outdoor activities like hiking, walking, or simply sitting in a quiet park can provide a much-needed break from the constant bombardment of noise. Nature's sounds have a unique way of shifting our focus away from internal and external noise, allowing us to reconnect with ourselves and the present moment.

Gardening

Gardening is another way to immerse yourself in nature. The act of nurturing plants is not only satisfying but can also be a quiet, contemplative activity that reduces stress and improves mood.

Physical Activity as a Noise Buffer

Physical activity is a powerful tool in silencing noise. When we engage our bodies, our minds often follow, shifting away from the chaos of noise to the rhythm of physical exertion. This transition from external noise to internal focus is a natural form of meditation that can bring about a sense of calm and clarity.

Aerobic Exercises

Activities like running, cycling, or swimming are not just good for physical health but also help clear your mind. They enable you to focus on your body's movements and breathing, providing a break from auditory distractions.

Yoga and Stretching

These gentle forms of exercise are particularly effective in quieting the mind. They combine physical movement with deep breathing and mindfulness, creating a perfect environment for internal silence.

Team Sports

Engaging in team sports can also be a great way to divert your attention from noise. The focus required in coordination and strategy in sports like basketball or soccer can help shift your attention away from distractions.

Creative Expression

Creative activities are not just hobbies; they are gateways to a quieter mind. When you're deeply engaged in a creative task, the noise around you fades into the background, allowing you to enter a state of "flow" where time and distractions seem to disappear.

Art and Craft

Drawing, painting, or crafting can be deeply meditative. As you focus on colors, textures, and designs, your mind shifts away from noise and into a space of creative expression.

Music

Playing a musical instrument or composing music can be an incredibly effective way to engage your mind fully and block out external noise. The concentration required to create or interpret music demands focus, pushing aside other distractions.

Writing

Whether it's journaling, poetry, or storytelling, writing is a powerful tool for introspection and expression. It allows you to articulate thoughts and emotions, providing a mental escape from noise and chaos.

Building a Routine

A well-structured routine can be a sanctuary from noise. It provides a framework that reduces the mental clutter of spontaneous decision-making and the stress of unplanned events. A routine establishes predictability in your day, creating pockets of quiet and focus.

Developing a Quiet Routine

Allocate specific times for activities like studying, exercising, and relaxing. Having a schedule can minimize the mental noise that comes from wondering what to do next.

Quiet Mornings

Starting your day with a quiet activity, such as meditation or a walk in nature, can set a peaceful tone for the rest of the day.

Evening Wind-Down

End your day with a routine that promotes relaxation, such as reading, gentle stretching, or listening to calming music. This can help quieten your mind and prepare you for a restful night's sleep (Oliver, 2023).

If noise is becoming a significant issue in your life, affecting your mental or emotional well-being, it's important to seek professional help. Schools often have counselors and mental health resources available. Don't hesitate to reach out if you feel overwhelmed by noise and its impact on your life. Integrating these methods into your daily routine can help foster a more serene, concentrated, and efficient personal space, even amidst the hustle and bustle of the external world. Remember, finding quiet isn't just about escaping noise; it's about nurturing your mental and emotional health, allowing you to thrive in all aspects of your life.

In Essence

In navigating the tumultuous and distraction-filled journey of adolescence, the mastery of selective hearing and mental clarity emerges as a pivotal skill, as elucidated in this chapter. It's a transformative approach that goes beyond seeking external silence, focusing instead on internal peace and concentration. This skill, rooted in the natural evolution of the teenage brain, is instrumental in fostering social skills, enhancing academic focus, and bolstering mental health. The chapter comprehensively outlines practical noise-blocking strategies, ranging from physical tools like earplugs and noise-canceling headphones to creating conducive environments and leveraging technology. It underscores the importance of internal tranquility through mindfulness and meditation, coupled with physical activities and creative pursuits, to achieve a mental state resistant to the chaos of the outside world. Establishing a routine further fortifies this serene environment, offering teenagers a sanctuary amidst the noise and guiding them toward a balanced and focused existence.

Chapter 6:

Immersion

Imagine yourself, headphones on, lost in the rhythm of your favorite song, oblivious to the world around you. Your foot taps in sync with the beat, your heart races with each crescendo, and for a moment, nothing else matters. This isn't just a simple escape; it's a deep dive into a world where they feel most alive, most themselves. This scene, familiar to many, exemplifies the essence of immersion—the heart of our journey in this exploration.

In our fast-paced, constantly connected world, finding that personal oasis of focused passion can seem like a Herculean task, especially for teenagers. The cacophony of school, social expectations, and the relentless pings of social media often drown out the inner voice that urges one to delve deeply into what truly ignites one's spirit. Yet, it is in these moments of deep engagement, where time seems to stand still and the outside world fades away, that we discover the purest form of pleasure and self-expression.

The concept of immersion extends far beyond just losing oneself in music or a hobby. It's about entering a state of flow, a term you might have heard tossed around but not fully understood. Is this flow state the same as immersion, or is it a gateway to achieving it? We'll explore this intriguing relationship, understanding how immersing ourselves in activities we love not only enriches our personal lives but also enhances our social connections.

Teenagers, especially, stand at a unique crossroads where the pursuit of personal interests often collides with the desire for social belonging. For those who identify as introverts, this journey can be even more nuanced. The stereotype of introverts as reclusive and antisocial is a misconception. In reality, introverts, much like extroverts, seek meaningful social connections; the difference lies in how they recharge and interact with the world. This chapter delves into the social benefits of immersion and how it can become a bridge to connect deeply with others, regardless of whether one is introverted or extroverted.

Understanding and embracing immersion in a flow state is not just about personal fulfillment; it's a tool for social integration and a testament to the diverse tapestry of human experience. It's about finding one's place in a world that often feels too loud, too fast, and too demanding. For teenagers seeking solace in their hobbies, passions, or interests, this journey of immersion is a powerful testament to the resilience and diversity of the human spirit. Let's embark on this journey together, understanding the challenges, unraveling the mysteries, and celebrating the joys of deep, passionate immersion.

What Is Immersion?

Immersion, a term often thrown around yet seldom explored in its full depth, is not merely a buzzword but a profound experience, especially for teenagers seeking to find their place in a world brimming with endless stimuli and distractions. At its core, immersion is about diving headfirst into an activity or interest, allowing it to envelop you completely to the point where everything else fades into the background. It's like putting on a pair of noise-canceling headphones on a busy street—suddenly, all you hear is the music, your own thoughts, and feelings.

For teenagers, this act of immersing oneself holds a special significance. It's not just about escaping the world; it's about finding a piece of it where they truly belong. In an age where one's sense of self is still forming, immersion can be a guiding light. It offers a space where passions ignite, talents are honed, and personalities are shaped. This deep engagement in activities they love—be it music, art, sports, or technology—provides a respite from the everyday challenges of teenage life, like academic pressures, social expectations, and the constant bombardment of social media.

But immersion is more than a personal journey; it has immense social benefits, too. When teenagers engage deeply in a hobby or interest, they often find themselves in communities of like-minded individuals. These spaces, whether physical like a sports team or virtual like an online gaming community, are melting pots of diverse backgrounds and experiences. In these settings, teenagers are not just sharing a hobby; they are sharing parts of their lives, their triumphs, and their struggles. This shared passion creates a bond that transcends typical social barriers of age, race, and geography.

In these immersive environments, teenagers learn invaluable social skills. They learn to communicate, to collaborate, and to be part of a team. They experience firsthand the joy of shared success and the lessons of collective failure. These are the arenas where friendships are forged in the fires of shared passion, where mentors emerge to guide young enthusiasts, and where teenagers find role models to inspire their own journeys.

Moreover, immersion in a community with shared interests can significantly boost a teenager's self-esteem and sense of belonging. It validates their interests and encourages them to explore and develop their skills further. This sense of achievement and belonging is crucial during the teenage years, a period often marred by self-doubt and a feeling of not fitting in.

Furthermore, immersion in a particular field or hobby often brings with it exposure to a variety of perspectives. Teenagers learn to appreciate and respect differences, understand the value of diversity, and develop a more inclusive worldview. This broadened perspective is invaluable in today's global society, where understanding and collaborating across cultures is more important than ever.

In essence, immersion for teenagers is not just a deep dive into a hobby or interest. It's a journey toward finding oneself and connecting with others on a level that transcends the superficial interactions of daily life. It's about building a network of support, inspiration, and friendship. In many ways, it is a foundational experience that shapes their understanding of themselves and their place in the world. The power of immersion lies not just in the personal fulfillment it brings but in its ability to connect teenagers more deeply with others who share their interests. It's a gateway to social integration, offering a unique blend of personal development and communal belonging. For teenagers navigating the complex waters of adolescence, immersion can be both an anchor and a sail, guiding them toward a more confident and connected future.

Immersion Into Flow State

At first glance, immersion might seem like just losing yourself in your favorite activity—be it gaming, playing music, or being engrossed in an enthralling book. However, it's more than just being involved; it's about being deeply engaged in a way that your entire focus is on that activity, and the rest of the world fades away. You might have experienced this while drawing something in art class or coding a new app, where time ceases to exist, and it's just you and your work.

Flow state, a term popularized by Mihaly Csikszentmihalyi, takes immersion a step further. Picture this: You're skateboarding, every turn and trick flowing seamlessly from one to the next, your mind and body in perfect harmony. Challenges exist, but they're just right—not too easy to be boring, not too hard to be frustrating. You're in a state of flow—fully immersed but also performing at your peak with a deep sense of satisfaction and accomplishment.

Are Immersion and Flow the Same?

While both immersion and flow involve deep engagement, they're not quite the same. Immersion is the first step—it's when you're fully absorbed in what you're doing. But flow is like reaching the peak of a mountain you've been climbing; it's when immersion meets challenge and skill in perfect balance. You're not just involved; you're excelling and enjoying it.

The Pathway From Immersion to Flow

Think of immersion as the gateway to flow. You first get deeply involved in an activity (immersion), and as you gain skills and face challenges that match these skills, you transition into a flow state. For instance, if you're learning a new language, you first immerse yourself in it—practicing, listening, and speaking. As you get better and the challenges increase (like having a conversation with a native speaker), you enter a flow state where learning feels effortless and enjoyable.

Why This Matters to You

Understanding and distinguishing between these states is crucial for you as a teenager. It's about finding what makes you tick, what challenges you, and what gives you that sense of fulfillment. It's about knowing that sometimes, when you're deeply involved in something, and it feels hard, you might just be on the cusp of entering a flow state—where true growth and enjoyment lie.

Harnessing the Power of Immersion and Flow

To harness these states in your life:

- **Identify your passions:** Start with activities that naturally interest you. It could be anything—music, sports, coding, writing, and so on.

- **Seek challenges:** As you get better, seek challenges that match your growing skills. If you love writing, try entering a writing contest.

- **Find balance:** Remember, too easy won't get you to flow, and too hard might discourage you. The key is finding that sweet spot where challenge meets skill.

- **Mindfulness and focus:** Practice being in the moment. Meditation and mindfulness can help you focus, a vital skill for achieving immersion and flow.

- **Feedback and growth:** Embrace feedback and view challenges as opportunities for growth. This mindset keeps you resilient and open to entering flow states.

- **Enjoy the process:** Lastly, remember to enjoy the journey. The joy of immersion and the rush of flow are rewards in themselves.

As you navigate the complex and exciting world of adolescence, understanding immersion and flow states can be your guide to finding deep enjoyment and peak performance in your pursuits. Whether it's acing a test, nailing a performance, or simply enjoying a hobby, these concepts can transform how you engage with the world.

Difficulties With Immersion

In the vivid tapestry of life, each of us, especially as teenagers, seeks to find that niche, that one activity or passion where we feel most at home. Immersion, the act of diving deep into an activity, subject, or interest, offers a gateway to such a personal haven. However, like any journey worth embarking upon, the path to true immersion is not without its challenges. Understanding these hurdles is essential, especially for teenagers navigating the complex landscapes of self-identity and skill development.

Challenge 1: Bridging the Skill Gap

Imagine you're standing at the edge of a vast canyon. On one side is your current skill level; on the other, the level you aspire to reach. This is the skill gap, a formidable chasm that every teenager must face on their journey to immersion. It's like wanting to play a soul-stirring melody on a guitar but only knowing a few basic chords. The gap between where you are and where you want to be can feel overwhelming.

How to overcome:

- **Set realistic goals:** Break down your ultimate goal into smaller, manageable steps. It's like learning a new language; start with common phrases before diving into complex grammar.

- **Practice regularly:** Consistency is key. Regular practice helps in gradually bridging the skill gap. Think of it as watering a plant regularly to see it flourish.

- **Seek guidance:** Don't hesitate to ask for help. Coaches, mentors, or online tutorials can provide invaluable insights and shortcuts to learning.

Challenge 2: The Clamor of Outside Noise

The world around us is a constant buzz of information, distractions, and expectations. For teenagers, this noise can be even louder. Social media, peer pressure, academic expectations, and family responsibilities constantly vie for attention, making it challenging to maintain focus on your chosen area of immersion.

How to overcome:

- **Create a dedicated space and time:** Just as a writer needs a quiet room, find or create a space where you can focus. Dedicate specific times for your activity, turning them into sacred, non-negotiable parts of your day.

- **Digital detox:** Limit the time spent on social media or other digital distractions. It's like putting blinders on a horse on a busy street, keeping you focused on the path ahead.

- **Mindfulness practices:** Techniques like meditation can enhance concentration, acting as a shield against the barrage of external noise.

Challenge 3: The Fear of Failure and Judgement

Many teenagers face the fear of not being good enough or being judged by others. This fear can be paralyzing, preventing you from taking risks or trying new things in your area of interest.

How to overcome:

- **Embrace failure as a learning tool:** Understand that failure is a stepping stone to mastery. Every great artist, scientist, or athlete has a history of setbacks that they use as lessons.

- **Develop a growth mindset:** Focus on personal improvement rather than comparison with others. Your journey is unique to you.

- **Build a supportive community:** Immerse yourself in an environment with individuals who uplift and back your passions. They are a source of inspiration and can offer valuable, constructive insights.

Challenge 4: Balancing Immersion With Other Responsibilities

As a teenager, you have various responsibilities—schoolwork, family duties, and social life. Balancing these with your passion can be like walking a tightrope.

How to overcome:

- **Effective time management:** Use tools like planners or apps to organize your schedule. Prioritize tasks and set aside dedicated time for your immersive activity.

- **Learn to say no:** It's okay to turn down activities or obligations that don't align with your goals. Remember, it's about quality, not quantity, of experiences.

- **Integrate your interests:** Where possible, integrate your passion with other aspects of your life. For example, if you're interested in photography, use it for school projects or family events.

The challenges you'll face are merely waves that you'll learn to navigate. Each hurdle, whether it's a skill gap, external distractions, fear of judgment, or balancing responsibilities, is an opportunity for growth and self-discovery. As you overcome these, you not only get closer to your passion but also build resilience, focus, and a deeper understanding of yourself.

In Essence

The journey toward immersion is a transformative expedition, especially for teenagers. It's a path filled with challenges, such as bridging the skill gap, silencing external distractions, overcoming the fear of judgment, and balancing various responsibilities. However, these challenges are not insurmountable barriers but rather stepping stones to personal growth and self-discovery. By setting realistic goals, practicing regularly, seeking guidance, and embracing a supportive community, teenagers can navigate these hurdles effectively. Immersion is more than just a deep engagement in a hobby or interest; it's a journey of finding one's own voice, building resilience, and connecting with a like-minded community. It's about harnessing the power of focused passion to carve out a niche in a noisy world. For teenagers, mastering this art of immersion is not just about achieving personal fulfillment; it's about shaping a confident, well-rounded, and connected future.

Chapter 7:

Crafts and Hobbies

Picture yourself sitting alone in your room, fingers deftly moving over a piece of clay, molding it into a shape only you can envision. There's a calmness that fills you, a sense of being completely in control of the creation unfolding before your eyes. This is your personal craft, a solitary activity where your imagination reigns supreme. Now, fast-forward to the weekend. You're in a bustling community center, laughter and chatter filling the air as you and a group of peers work on a giant mural. The energy is different; it's collaborative and, somehow, just as fulfilling as your solo project.

This is the essence of what we're delving into in this exploration of crafts and hobbies. It's not just about the activities themselves; it's about the balance between personal satisfaction and social interaction that these activities bring. We often hear about the importance of "finding a balance" in life, but what does that really look like for a teenager? Here, we're going to unravel that mystery.

Our journey starts with "Personal Crafts." What does it mean to engage in an activity solely for yourself? It could be painting, writing, knitting, or any other activity that allows you to dive deep into your own world. These are moments where you're not just creating something beautiful or interesting; you're also building a deeper understanding of yourself.

As we explore these realms, remember that the activities you choose should resonate with you. They should feed your inner desires, not just be a means to an end. Choosing an activity solely for social reasons might leave you feeling disconnected. It's about finding what genuinely interests you, be it a mentally stimulating game of chess or the physical exertion of sports.

This journey is not just about hobbies; it's about discovering and balancing different aspects of your personality. It's about finding joy in solitude as well as in company. As you navigate through these paths, you'll find yourself growing, not just in your skills but in your confidence and your ability to interact with the world around you. So, let's dive in and explore the wonderful world of crafts and hobbies and find the perfect balance that makes you, well, you.

Personal Crafts

Embarking on a journey of personal crafts and activities can be an enlightening and enriching experience, especially for teenagers seeking to discover their interests and talents. When you're alone, the world of personal crafts opens up a spectrum of possibilities, enabling you to delve into activities that not only pass the time but also contribute to your personal growth and creativity. Let's explore some engaging crafts and activities you can immerse yourself in when you're spending time with yourself.

Creative Writing

Writing is a powerful tool for self-expression. It's not just about penning down stories or poems; it's about unleashing your imagination. You could start a journal, write short stories, or even start your own blog. The beauty of writing is that there are no boundaries. You can create entire worlds, dive into the depths of your feelings, or simply document your day-to-day experiences. Moreover, it helps improve your communication skills, which are valuable assets in any career.

Sketching and Drawing

Engaging in drawing and sketching offers a fantastic avenue for visually conveying your ideas. It's not necessary to have innate artistic talent to relish in this activity. Begin with basic sketches, such as doodling characters you like or capturing scenes from nature. Over time, you might find your unique style. This hobby is not only calming but also enhances your observation skills and attention to detail and can be a great way to communicate ideas visually.

DIY Projects

The world of "Do It Yourself" (DIY) is vast and varied. From creating your room decor to upcycling old clothes, the possibilities are endless. Projects like making a dream catcher, customizing your denim jacket with patches, or creating handmade gifts for friends and family can be incredibly fulfilling. These projects not only foster creativity but also teach you the value of resourcefulness and sustainability.

Photography

Photography is a powerful medium to capture the world through your lens. It could be as simple as taking photos with your phone or using a camera if you have access to one. Experiment with different angles, lighting, and subjects. It's a fantastic way to document your life and see the beauty in everyday moments. Plus, it helps you develop a keen eye for detail and aesthetics.

Cooking and Baking

The kitchen can be a laboratory for delicious experiments. Cooking or baking can be immensely satisfying—it's like chemistry but with flavors and aromas. Start with simple recipes and gradually move to more complex ones. This not only results in delicious outcomes but also teaches you about different cultures, patience, and the joy of creating something from scratch.

Music

If you have a passion for music, exploring it can be therapeutic. You could learn to play an instrument, write songs, or even produce music digitally. Music is a universal language that allows you to express emotions that words cannot. It also enhances your cognitive abilities and can be a great way to connect with others who share similar interests.

Gardening

Gardening, even if it's just a small plant in your room, can be incredibly grounding and rewarding. It teaches you responsibility, as taking care of plants requires regular attention. Watching something grow because of your care is a beautiful, fulfilling experience. Plus, it connects you to nature, which can be a great stress reliever.

Knitting or Crocheting

The rhythmic nature of knitting or crocheting can be almost meditative. Creating something wearable or usable out of yarn can be incredibly satisfying. This pastime is an excellent method for unwinding, and as a bonus, you create something tangible, whether it's a scarf, a hat, or a warm blanket.

Learning Online

The internet is a treasure trove of learning opportunities. You can learn practically anything online—from coding and digital art to foreign languages and science. Platforms like Coursera, Khan Academy, or YouTube offer endless resources. This not only keeps you engaged but also enhances your resume and prepares you for future career opportunities.

Mindfulness and Meditation

Engaging in mindfulness or meditation can be a profoundly effective means of establishing a connection with oneself. It involves being fully present in the moment and gaining insight into your thoughts and emotions. This can lead to greater self-awareness, reduced stress, and a more balanced approach to life's challenges.

Embarking on a journey of personal crafts when alone is not just about keeping yourself busy. It's about self-discovery, learning new skills, and expressing your creativity. Each activity offers its unique benefits and can contribute significantly to your personal development.

Social Hobbies

In a world where digital screens often dominate our time, engaging in social hobbies offers a refreshing way to connect with others and develop essential interpersonal skills. For teenagers, these activities are more than just pastimes; they're opportunities to explore interests, build friendships, and learn valuable life skills. Let's dive into a variety of social hobbies that are perfect for teens seeking meaningful and enjoyable interactions.

Music and Performing Arts

Whether you're into rock, pop, jazz, or classical, joining or forming a band is a fantastic way to meet people with similar musical tastes. Collaborating on songs, practicing for performances, and even writing music together can foster deep connections.

Similarly, participating in drama activities isn't just for aspiring actors. It's a great space to express yourself, understand diverse perspectives, and work collaboratively on productions. From acting to stage management, there's a role for everyone.

Visual Arts and Crafts

Joining art classes or workshops in your community can be both relaxing and socially engaging. Whether it's painting, sculpting, or digital art, these classes often foster a supportive environment for creativity and conversation. Additionally, initiating or becoming part of a DIY craft group offers an enjoyable opportunity to acquire new skills and exchange creative ideas. Projects can range from simple crafts to elaborate designs, providing a sense of accomplishment and community.

Outdoor and Nature Activities

If you love the outdoors, joining a hiking or camping group is a fantastic way to meet others who share your passion. These activities not only offer exercise and fresh air but also provide unique bonding experiences in nature. Similarly, engaging in environmental advocacy or conservation projects can be deeply fulfilling. Working alongside others to protect nature can spark lifelong friendships and a shared sense of purpose.

Sports and Physical Activities

Sports like soccer, basketball, or volleyball are great for building teamwork skills and forming friendships. Even if you're not the most athletic, there's a sense of camaraderie and achievement in playing together. Furthermore, whether it's hip-hop, ballet, or contemporary dance, joining a dance class is a lively way to connect with others. It's not just about the steps; it's about the shared experience and expression.

Academic and Skill-Based Clubs

Joining a debate team or a public speaking club can be incredibly rewarding. It sharpens your communication skills and introduces you to others who enjoy intellectual discussions and friendly debates.

Similarly, learning a new language with a group provides a supportive environment to practice and learn from each other's mistakes. It's also a great way to prepare for travel or future studies.

Volunteer Work and Community Service

Engaging in community service, like helping at a food bank or organizing charity events, is not only altruistic but also a chance to work with a diverse group of people united by a common goal. Moreover, offering your skills as a tutor in subjects you excel in is a meaningful way to connect with peers. It's a two-way street of learning and sharing knowledge.

Social hobbies offer more than just fun; they're gateways to new experiences, friendships, and personal growth. For teens, these activities are especially crucial as they provide a safe and structured environment to explore interests, develop social skills, and build networks that can last a lifetime. Whether it's through art, sports, volunteering, or any other group activity, the experiences gained from these hobbies can shape your character and future in profound ways.

Social Hobbies and Personal Crafts

Taking up hobbies and crafts goes beyond merely occupying time; it's about enhancing your life in a manner that personally resonates with you. Whether it's the tranquility of painting, the strategic depth of chess, or the physical exhilaration of sports, your choice of activity should fundamentally satisfy your inner yearnings and interests. As teenagers, you're at a crucial stage of self-discovery, and your hobbies can play a pivotal role in this journey.

The Social Dimension of Hobbies

While personal fulfillment is key, don't overlook the social aspect of certain activities. Hobbies like theater, sports, or even group-oriented video games offer more than just fun; they serve as conduits for connecting with others. Shared interests naturally foster social interactions, helping you build friendships and networks that could last a lifetime.

Introverts and Extroverts

If you lean toward introversion, hobbies that stimulate your mind, like chess or coding, might be more appealing. These activities offer the dual benefits of solitude and mental engagement. However, occasionally stepping into more socially demanding hobbies like sports or drama can offer unexpected joys. They push you out of your comfort zone, potentially unlocking new facets of your personality and skill set.

Extroverts, on the other hand, might naturally gravitate toward team sports or social clubs. These environments thrive on interaction and teamwork, fitting perfectly with an extrovert's energy. However, incorporating quieter, more introspective hobbies like reading or crafting can provide a healthy balance, offering moments of reflection and personal growth.

Balancing Acts

The key is balance. Diving into a social hobby just for the sake of fitting in or meeting a social quota can backfire, leading to disinterest or even resentment toward the activity. It's about finding that sweet spot—a hobby or craft that aligns with your interests, challenges you in a good way, and maybe, just maybe, helps you connect with others on a deeper level.

Personal Growth Through Hobbies

As you explore and balance these activities, you'll likely notice a positive shift in yourself. Your social skills might sharpen, your confidence could soar, and your understanding of teamwork and collaboration may deepen. All these skills are vital as you navigate through your teenage years and beyond. Remember, the journey of discovering the right mix of hobbies and crafts is uniquely yours. It's a path of trial and error, of self-discovery, and of unexpected joys. Embrace it with an open mind, and let your interests and passions guide you. Whether you're an introvert, extrovert, or somewhere in between, there's a world of activities waiting for you—each offering its own unique blend of personal satisfaction and social connection.

In Essence

For teenagers, engaging in hobbies and crafts is a crucial aspect of growth, offering a mix of personal discovery and social interaction. Personal activities like writing, drawing, or crafting provide a sanctuary for self-expression and creativity, fostering introspection and a deep connection with one's inner self. On the other hand, social hobbies such as music, sports, or volunteering are not just fun; they're essential for developing teamwork, empathy, and communication skills, building friendships, and creating a sense of community. The key to a fulfilling teenage experience lies in balancing these two worlds: the quiet, introspective realm of personal crafts and the vibrant, communal space of social activities. This balance helps teenagers not only discover and nurture their passions and interests but also develop the crucial life skills of self-reliance and social adeptness, paving the way for a well-rounded and confident adulthood.

Chapter 8:

Defining Yourself

Imagine you're in a library, surrounded by shelves towering with books. Each book tells a different story, a unique experience, and a distinct voice. Now, imagine you're one of those books. Your cover might not scream for attention, and your spine might blend in with the others, but inside, your pages are rich with thoughts, dreams, and a depth that's uniquely yours. This is the essence of being an introvert in an extroverted world. It's about understanding and embracing the story written in your pages, a journey of self-discovery that's as quietly profound as the world within those library walls.

Passion for an introvert can be like a secret chapter in your book, one that's filled with vibrant imagery and compelling narratives. It's what makes your eyes light up and your spirit soar. In this chapter, we'll explore how to turn these pages of passion into a driving force, a beacon that guides you through the quiet yet profound journey of self-discovery.

The process of understanding yourself is akin to reading through your own chapters, understanding each line, and appreciating the nuances. It's about building a life that suits your narrative, one that respects your need for introspection and deep thinking. We'll delve into how you can create systems and strategies that align with your introverted nature, ensuring that your journey is both fulfilling and sustainable.

Then, we focus on the outcome—the production of your journey. This isn't just about what you achieve outwardly but how you grow inwardly. We'll explore how the intangible results, like self-awareness and inner peace, are as significant as the tangible ones. This section is about seeing the value in every aspect of your growth and the unique impact you make in the world.

This chapter is a gentle reminder that understanding yourself is a lifelong journey. There's no timeline or specific endpoint. It's a path of continuous discovery and growth. Being introverted isn't a limitation; it's a perspective that adds depth and richness to your story. Every step forward, no matter how small, is a valuable part of your narrative.

Passion: Igniting Your Fire

Passion is a powerful force akin to a fire burning within you. It's not just about liking something; it's about feeling deeply connected to it. For teenagers, passion can be found in various forms, whether it's art, science, sports, or social causes. It's something that makes your eyes light up when you talk about it, that thing you can spend hours working on without feeling tired. It's your own unique spark that sets you apart.

Discovering and Nurturing Your Passion

Finding your passion might not happen overnight. It often requires exploration and an open mind. Try new things, whether it's a sport, a subject in school, a musical instrument, or a form of art. Pay attention to what excites you, what challenges you in a good way, and what you daydream about. Once you find your passion, nurture it. Read about it, practice it, talk to others who share it, and look for opportunities to grow it. Remember, your passion is like a fire—it needs fuel to keep burning. This fuel can be your curiosity, dedication, and the joy you derive from engaging in your passion.

Process

To harness your passion and channel it effectively, you need to set up systems and routines. Begin by setting clear, achievable goals. What do you want to achieve with your passion? Break it down into smaller, manageable tasks. For example, if your passion is writing, set a goal to write a certain number of words each day.

Time Management and Prioritization

As a teenager, you're juggling school, hobbies, social life, and maybe even part-time work. Effective time management is crucial. Prioritize tasks and use tools like planners or apps to keep track of your schedule. Don't forget to allocate time for relaxation and socializing—these are just as important for your overall well-being.

Healthy Habits

Your physical and mental health are foundational to your success. Ensure you're getting enough sleep, eating nutritious foods, and engaging in physical activities. Mental health is equally important, so practice stress-reduction techniques like meditation, deep breathing exercises, or simply engaging in activities that bring you joy and relaxation (Newsom & Rehman, 2020).

Production

Success isn't just about winning awards or getting recognition. It's also about personal growth, the skills you've developed, and the joy your passion brings you. Reflect on what you've learned and how you've grown since you started pursuing your passion. Have you become more confident? More skilled? More knowledgeable?

Seeking Feedback and Continuing to Grow

To improve further, seek feedback from mentors, teachers, peers, or professionals in your field of interest. Constructive criticism can be a powerful tool for growth. Don't be discouraged by setbacks or negative feedback; instead, use it as a stepping stone to get better.

Expanding Your Horizons

Finally, keep looking for opportunities to expand your knowledge and skills. This might mean taking advanced classes, joining clubs or teams, participating in competitions, or finding internships. Keep an open mind to new experiences that can enhance your understanding and execution of your passion.

Your journey through passion, process, and production is unique and ever-evolving. Embrace each step, celebrate your achievements, and always be open to learning and growing. Remember, the most successful people are those who find a way to do what they love.

Pursuing Your Passion as an Introvert

As a teenager, understanding and accepting your introverted nature is crucial. Introversion isn't a barrier to success; it's a unique lens through which you see the world. Introverts often enjoy solitude, introspection, and deep thinking. These qualities are not limitations but strengths that can propel you toward achieving your dreams. Passion is the fire that ignites your potential. It's about finding something that excites you, something that makes you leap out of bed each morning with enthusiasm. This could be anything from art, science, and technology to social causes. Your passion is your compass, guiding you through life's journey.

Navigating Social Challenges as an Introverted Teen

The teenage years can be socially challenging, especially for introverts. School environments, with their emphasis on group activities and social interactions, might feel overwhelming. Remember, it's okay to step back and recharge when you need to. Seek out like-minded peers who share your interests and passions. They can become your support system, helping you navigate the social complexities of teenage life.

Creating Your Comfort Zone

Your comfort zone is where your creativity and passion thrive. For introverted teens, this might mean working in quieter, more controlled environments. Don't hesitate to create a space where you feel most at ease, whether it's a corner of your room, a spot in the library, or a quiet park.

Balancing Solitude and Social Interactions

While solitude is essential for introverts, occasional social interactions are equally important. Engaging with others can provide new perspectives, inspiration, and opportunities to share your passion. Try joining clubs or groups that align with your interests. This can be a less intimidating way of interacting with peers while staying true to your introverted nature.

Managing Energy Levels

As an introvert, social interactions can be draining. It's crucial to manage your energy wisely. Schedule downtime after social activities to recharge. Balance your school life with activities that nurture your inner world, like reading, writing, or simply enjoying nature.

Embracing Technology and Online Communities

The digital world offers a haven for introverted teens. Online communities can be a great way to connect with others who share your passions without the energy drain of face-to-face interactions. Engage in forums, follow blogs, and participate in online workshops to expand your knowledge and network.

The Introvert's Advantage in Pursuing Passion

Introverts often have the advantage of deep focus and the ability to work independently for extended periods. Use these traits to dive deep into your areas of interest. Research, create, experiment, and learn at your own pace.

Overcoming Fear and Building Confidence

It's normal to feel hesitant or fearful when stepping out of your comfort zone. Start with small steps. Share your work or ideas with close friends or family before presenting them to a larger audience. Celebrate small victories and gradually build your confidence.

Preparing for the Future

As you pursue your passion, think about how it might shape your future. Explore careers and fields that align with your interests. Seek out mentors or role models who can guide you. Remember, your introverted nature can be a powerful asset in many professional fields.

Being an introvert is not just about who you are; it's about how you uniquely engage with the world. Your passion, coupled with your introspective nature, can lead to profound creativity and innovation. Embrace your introversion, follow your passion, and remember that your journey is uniquely yours. Remember, in a world that often celebrates extroversion, your introverted qualities are not just valuable but essential.

Embracing Your Introversion While Fueling Your Passion

As an introvert, you possess a unique set of qualities that shape who you are. This doesn't mean you're destined to live a life on the sidelines; rather, it's an opportunity to engage with the world in a way that honors your natural tendencies. Recognizing and respecting your introverted nature is the first step toward a fulfilling life where you can thrive without feeling overwhelmed.

Balancing Social Engagement With Personal Boundaries

While it's beneficial to engage in activities and social interactions, it's equally important to do so on your own terms. As an introvert, large groups or extended socializing can be draining. Therefore, developing strategies to participate without pushing yourself to the point of exhaustion is key. This might mean setting time limits for social events or choosing activities that align with your interests, allowing you to enjoy the company of others in a more comfortable setting.

The Intangible and Tangible Rewards of Self-Understanding

Your journey as an introvert will yield both visible and invisible rewards. On the tangible side, you might find yourself forming deeper connections with a select group of friends or discovering hobbies and interests that bring you joy and satisfaction. The intangible rewards, however, are just as important. These include setting boundaries that protect your energy and time and developing a deep sense of self-respect and understanding.

The Ongoing Journey of Self-Discovery

Remember, defining yourself is not a race; it's a lifelong journey. Many people spend years, even their entire lives, trying to understand themselves. As a teenager, you're at the beginning of this exciting journey. It's okay to start by understanding just parts of who you are. Each insight you gain about your introverted nature is a step towards a fuller, more authentic self.

Introversion Is Not a Barrier to Personal Growth

Being introverted is not a limitation; it's simply a characteristic of your personality. It's important to challenge yourself and step out of your comfort zone, but always in ways that feel right for you. Personal growth and development are not exclusive to extroverts. As an introvert, you have the opportunity to grow in depth and introspection, developing a rich inner life that can be just as rewarding as any external achievement.

As an introverted teenager, embrace the unique qualities that make you who you are. Use your introversion as a strength, not a hindrance. By respecting your needs and boundaries, engaging in activities that align with your personality, and taking the time to understand yourself, you'll build a life that's not only successful but also deeply satisfying.

In Essence

In the grand tapestry of life, the journey of an introverted teenager is akin to a rich yet understated narrative in a world that often prizes extroversion. This path is not just about navigating an extroverted world but about thriving within it by embracing the depth and introspection unique to introverts. It involves discovering and nurturing a passion that ignites the spirit, developing personalized systems and strategies for sustainable growth, and balancing introspection with external achievements. The true essence of this journey lies in appreciating both the tangible and intangible outcomes—self-awareness, confidence, inner peace—and recognizing that each step, no matter how small, is a profound contribution to their unique story. This journey, marked by introspective depth and thoughtful progression, celebrates the quiet yet impactful presence of introverted teens in a world that often overlooks the power of quiet introspection.

Chapter 9:

Congratulations, Strength

Achieved!

Think about a scenario. You're standing at the edge of a cliff, gazing into a vast, open sky. Your heart races with a mix of fear and exhilaration. This is it—the moment of truth. You've climbed this mountain, step by arduous step, overcoming obstacles that once seemed insurmountable. Now, as you stand here, ready to leap into the unknown, you realize something profound: You're no longer the person who started this journey. You've transformed and evolved. Your strength, once hidden, now shines like a beacon.

This moment is a metaphor for where you are in your life. You've journeyed through the twists and turns of adolescence, each challenge shaping you into a stronger, more resilient person. But what does this newfound strength mean for your future? How do you harness it to shape the life you want?

As you've traveled this path, you've learned to embody internal strength. It's not just a feeling inside you; it's visible to everyone around you. Your friends, your family, and even your teachers have noticed a change. There's a new confidence in your stride, a new clarity in your eyes.

Now, you might be wondering, *What now*? You recognize your strength, but what do you do with it? This isn't the end of your journey; it's just the beginning. A beginning where you build on this strength, exploring its depths and testing its limits.

You'll start to notice this strength manifesting in everything you do. It's in the way you speak, the way you tackle problems, and the way you face your fears. It's in the small moments, like standing up for a friend, and in the big ones, like making life-changing decisions.

But remember, building on your strength requires patience. You never really know the full extent of your strength until you're tested. And life, as you know, has a way of throwing tests your way. It's in these moments that you'll discover just how strong you are.

One effective way to understand and use your strengths is by performing a SWOT analysis. This tool helps you identify not only your strengths but also your weaknesses, opportunities, and threats (Kenton, 2023). It's a way of taking stock of how far you've come and mapping out where you want to go.

So, as you stand on this metaphorical cliff, ready to leap, remember this: Your journey of self-discovery and strength is a never-ending one. Each day brings new challenges but also new opportunities to grow and shine. Embrace it with the knowledge that you are stronger than you ever imagined.

What Now?

You've discovered your inner strength, a remarkable journey of resilience and self-awareness. But what comes next? How do you harness this newfound power and grow even further? This guide is tailored for teenagers like you, who are ready to embark on a journey of personal development, building upon the strong foundation they've already established.

Understanding Your Strength

Understanding your strengths is a crucial aspect of personal growth, particularly during the transformative teenage years. It's about recognizing and harnessing your unique capabilities and resilience. This understanding forms the foundation upon which you can build a fulfilling and successful life.

Recognizing Your Strengths and Weaknesses

The journey begins with a deep dive into self-discovery. You need to identify your strengths—these could be traits like empathy, creativity, determination, or a particular skill set such as excellent communication, problem-solving, or artistic talents. It's not just about acknowledging what you are good at; it's also crucial to understand how these strengths manifest in your daily life. For instance, your creativity might shine when you're brainstorming for a school project or when you're finding solutions to problems in your personal life. Conversely, understanding your weaknesses is equally important. Weaknesses aren't failures; they're opportunities for growth. Perhaps you struggle with time management, get easily stressed in certain situations, or find it challenging to understand complex mathematical problems. Recognizing these areas isn't to discourage you but to empower you with the knowledge of where your growth can occur.

To truly understand your strengths and weaknesses, you might want to engage in activities like personality tests, feedback sessions with friends, family, or teachers, and self-reflection through journaling. Remember, this process is about gaining a holistic view of who you are, not just a list of traits.

Reflecting on Your Experiences

Reflection is a powerful tool for understanding your inner strength. It involves looking back at your life experiences, both positive and negative, and analyzing them (Gupta, 2023). What challenges have you faced, and how did you overcome them? What successes have you achieved, and what did you learn from them? Engaging in this process is more than just reflecting on the past; it involves proactively searching for the lessons embedded in each experience. For instance, think about a time when you failed at something important to you. Reflecting on this experience isn't just about acknowledging the failure but understanding what it taught you. Did it make you more resilient? Did it teach you the importance of preparation or the value of seeking help?

Reflection also involves recognizing patterns in your behavior. Do you tend to give up when faced with difficulty, or do you persist until you find a solution? Understanding these patterns is key to leveraging your strengths and addressing your weaknesses.

Embracing Self-Awareness

Embracing self-awareness is about more than just knowing your likes and dislikes; it's about understanding your core values, motivations, emotional responses, and how you interact with the world around you. It's a critical step in personal development, especially for teenagers whose identities are still evolving.

Deepening Self-Understanding

To deepen your self-understanding, start by exploring your values and beliefs. What matters most to you? Is it family, honesty, creativity, independence, or something else? Understanding your values helps you make decisions that are aligned with your true self. Next, consider your motivations. What drives you to do well in school, participate in sports, or engage in your favorite hobbies? Understanding your motivations helps you harness them more effectively and guides you toward activities and goals that are genuinely fulfilling.

Another aspect of deepening self-understanding is recognizing your emotional patterns. How do you typically react to stress, success, failure, or conflict? Do you withdraw, seek support, or confront the issue head-on? Understanding these patterns is key to managing your emotions constructively.

Cultivating Mindfulness and Reflection

Mindfulness and reflection are powerful tools for developing self-awareness. Mindfulness involves staying present and fully engaging with the here and now. This practice aids in increasing your awareness of your thoughts, emotions, and responses as they happen. Practices like meditation, mindful breathing, and yoga can enhance your mindfulness.

Reflection, on the other hand, involves looking inward and contemplating your thoughts, feelings, and behaviors. It can be practiced through journaling, quiet contemplation, or even through art. Reflecting on your day, your interactions with others, and your responses to various situations provides deeper insights into your inner self.

Seeking Feedback and Perspective

Feedback from others can be invaluable in developing self-awareness. Sometimes, it's hard to see ourselves objectively, and the perspective of others can provide new insights. Seek feedback from family, friends, teachers, or mentors. Ask them about your strengths, areas for improvement, how you handle stress, and how you interact in social situations. However, it's important to approach this feedback with an open mind and a willingness to consider it constructively. Not all feedback will be easy to hear, but it's all valuable in the journey toward self-awareness.

Engaging in Continuous Self-Exploration

Self-awareness is not a destination; it's a continuous journey. As you grow and have new experiences, your understanding of yourself will evolve. Regularly engage in self-exploration activities, whether it's trying new things, pushing your boundaries, or revisiting your goals and values. This ongoing process helps you stay in tune with yourself, even as you change and grow.

Setting Personal Goals

Setting personal goals is a crucial step in building on your inner strength. It involves envisioning your future, determining what you want to achieve, and outlining a path to reach those achievements. This process not only provides direction and purpose but also fuels motivation and personal fulfillment.

Defining Clear Objectives

The foundation of setting personal goals is to define what you truly want to achieve. This clarity is vital for directing your efforts and resources effectively. Goals can vary widely, from academic achievements to personal development objectives, such as improving communication skills or learning a new language.

- **Self-reflection:** Start by reflecting on your interests, passions, and aspirations. What activities make you feel most alive? Where do you see yourself in the future? Such self-reflection can assist you in pinpointing aspects of your life where you aspire to develop or skills you desire to learn.

- **Specificity:** Ensure your goals are specific. Instead of setting a vague goal like "get better at math," aim for something more concrete, such as "improve my math grade to a B+ in the next semester."

- **Realism:** While it's good to challenge yourself, your goals should be realistic and attainable. Setting an unachievable goal can lead to disappointment and demotivation.

- **Time-bound:** Assign a timeline to your goals. Whether it's short-term goals like completing a project in a week or long-term goals like mastering a musical instrument in a year, timelines create a sense of urgency and help in tracking progress.

Breaking Down Goals

Breaking down your goals into smaller, more manageable tasks makes them less daunting and easier to tackle. This approach provides a clear roadmap and helps maintain focus and motivation.

- **Actionable steps:** Divide each goal into actionable steps. For example, if your goal is to write a novel, start by setting smaller tasks such as outlining the plot, developing characters, and writing a certain number of words each day.

- **Prioritization:** Some goals or tasks will be more important or time-sensitive than others. Prioritize these to ensure you're focusing on the most critical aspects of your goal.

- **Consistent review:** Regularly review and adjust your goals as needed. Life is dynamic, and your goals may need to adapt to new circumstances or insights gained along the way.

- **Celebrating milestones:** Recognize and celebrate when you achieve a milestone. This acknowledgment serves as a positive reinforcement, encouraging you to continue pursuing your goals.

- **Learning from setbacks:** Understand that setbacks are part of the process. Instead of being discouraged, analyze what went wrong and how you can avoid similar issues in the future.

Developing Emotional Intelligence

Emotional intelligence is the ability to understand, use, and manage your emotions in positive ways to relieve stress, communicate effectively, empathize with others, overcome challenges, and defuse conflict. Developing emotional intelligence is fundamental for personal growth and building strong relationships (Segal et al., 2023).

Understanding Your Emotions

Recognizing and understanding your emotions is the first step in developing emotional intelligence. This self-awareness allows you to navigate through your feelings without being overwhelmed by them.

- **Identifying emotions:** Learn to identify and name your emotions. Are you feeling anxious, frustrated, excited, or sad? Being able to put a label on your feelings is crucial in understanding and managing them.

- **Triggers and responses:** Pay attention to what triggers certain emotions. What situations, people, or events evoke strong reactions? Understanding these triggers can help you prepare and respond more effectively.

- **Journaling:** Maintaining a journal serves as an efficient method for monitoring your emotions and identifying the situations that provoke them. Over time, patterns may emerge that can offer insights into your emotional responses.

- **Mindfulness and reflection:** Practice mindfulness and take time to reflect on your feelings. Mindfulness techniques, such as meditation, can help you stay centered and give you a clearer perspective on your emotions.

Practicing Empathy

Empathy is the ability to understand and share the feelings of others. It's a key component of emotional intelligence, as it enhances your ability to connect with people on a deeper level (Reid, 2023).

- **Active listening:** Listen to others with the intent to understand, not just to reply. Pay attention to their words, tone of voice, and body language. This attentiveness shows that you value their perspective.

- **Perspective-taking:** Try to see situations from others' viewpoints. This practice can help you understand their reactions and emotions better, fostering deeper connections.

- **Empathetic communication:** Communicate your understanding of others' feelings. Phrases like "I see that you're upset because..." or "It sounds like you're feeling..." can validate their emotions and build trust.

- **Self-regulation in relationships:** Be aware of how your emotions and behavior impact others. Practice self-regulation to ensure that your responses are considerate and conducive to healthy relationships.

Managing Emotions in Challenging Situations

Developing emotional intelligence also involves managing your emotions effectively, especially in difficult or stressful situations. Learning stress management techniques such as deep breathing, progressive muscle relaxation, or visualization is invaluable (Toussaint et al., 2021). These methods can help calm your mind, providing clarity in stressful situations. It's essential to find constructive outlets for your emotions. Engaging in creative activities like art and writing or physical activities such as sports or exercise can be highly beneficial.

It's also crucial not to hesitate in seeking support when needed. Talking to a trusted friend, family member, or counselor can offer a different perspective and assist in navigating challenging emotions. Developing emotional agility is another key aspect. This means being flexible with your emotions and adapting to changing situations without being rigid in your emotional responses. Furthermore, learning effective conflict-resolution skills is essential. Understanding and managing emotions can play a crucial role in resolving disagreements and maintaining healthy relationships. Lastly, utilizing empathy during conflicts can be a game-changer. Trying to understand the other person's point of view can de-escalate tensions and lead to more productive resolutions.

Developing emotional intelligence is a journey that requires patience, practice, and self-compassion. It enhances your ability to connect with others, manage stress, and navigate the complexities of emotional experiences. By setting clear, achievable personal goals and consistently working toward them, you build discipline, focus, and a sense of accomplishment. Together, these skills form a robust framework for personal growth and resilience, equipping you to face life's challenges with confidence and grace.

Enhancing Social Connections

In the journey of personal growth and building inner strength, the role of social connections cannot be overstated. Strong relationships, whether with family, friends, or mentors, provide a support system, offer different perspectives, and contribute to our emotional and mental well-being.

Nurturing Relationships

Building and maintaining positive relationships is an art that involves empathy, understanding, and communication. Learning to express yourself clearly and actively listen is crucial for effective communication. It's not just about speaking; it's equally about listening and understanding others. Spending quality time with those close to you is also important. Engage in activities you and your friends or family members enjoy, whether it's a shared meal, a walk in the park, or a movie night.

Being there for others in times of need and offering support and encouragement is essential. You'll often find this support reciprocated. Understanding and respecting that everyone is different is key. Embracing these differences can broaden your perspective and understanding of the world.

Building trust is fundamental in any strong relationship. Be reliable, keep your promises, and show that you can be trusted. Learning to handle disagreements in a healthy way is vital. Avoid blame and look for solutions that are agreeable to all parties involved. Finally, showing appreciation for your friends and family is important. A simple "thank you" can go a long way in strengthening relationships.

Seeking Mentors

Mentors are crucial in personal development, offering guidance and advice based on their experiences and opening doors to new opportunities. When identifying a mentor, look for someone who embodies the qualities you aspire to develop. This individual could be a teacher, coach, family member, or a professional in your field of interest.

Approach potential mentors with respect and sincerity. Building a meaningful relationship involves showing genuine interest in their work and seeking their advice or guidance. Being receptive to feedback is also essential. Open yourself to constructive criticism, as a mentor's insight can be invaluable in identifying areas for improvement. Maintaining regular interaction with your mentor is important. This can be through meetings, phone calls, or email exchanges. Applying the lessons learned from your mentor is crucial. Demonstrate to them that their guidance is being valued and utilized for your growth.

Networking is another significant aspect of having a mentor. Utilize the opportunity to expand your network through your mentor, who can introduce you to new people, ideas, and opportunities. Finally, giving back is a vital part of the mentoring process. In time, you can also become a mentor to others, passing on the knowledge and experience you have gained.

Cultivating a Growth Mindset

Developing a growth mindset is fundamental to building inner strength. It involves seeing challenges as opportunities, learning from failures, and believing in your ability to grow and improve (Smith, 2020).

Embracing Challenges

Embracing challenges as opportunities for growth is a transformative approach. Adopting a positive attitude toward difficult situations enables you to see them as valuable chances to learn and develop. Regular engagement in activities that push you beyond your comfort zone is beneficial. This could involve trying a new sport, speaking in public, or taking on a challenging project.

Actively seeking out challenges is also important. Rather than waiting for them to arise, proactively take on tasks that you find intimidating or difficult. Maintaining a positive attitude in the face of challenges is crucial. Remind yourself that each challenge presents an opportunity to learn something new.

Developing resilience is key. It's important not to give up when faced with setbacks. Learning to bounce back stronger from each difficulty is a vital skill. Reflecting on past challenges and the lessons learned is also essential. Use these insights to approach future challenges more effectively, continuously improving your ability to handle and grow from difficult situations.

Learning From Failures

Understanding that failure is a natural and integral part of the learning process is essential. It's important to recognize that failing does not define you as a failure; instead, it contributes to making you wiser and stronger. Accepting failure as a part of growth is crucial. It's vital not to berate yourself over mistakes or setbacks but to view them as steps in your learning journey. Taking time to analyze your failures is equally important. Understand what went wrong and how you can avoid similar mistakes in the future.

Being open to constructive criticism following a failure is beneficial. This criticism can offer valuable insights and areas for improvement. It's also important not to fear failure. The fear of failure can be paralyzing and can prevent you from trying new things and taking risks that could lead to growth.

Cultivating resilience when confronted with failure is crucial. Persisting through setbacks, with the understanding that each failure is a step toward eventual success, is essential. Celebrating small wins after a setback is also helpful. This maintains a positive attitude and motivation, which is essential for continued effort and growth. Lastly, seeking support from friends, family, or mentors when dealing with failure is important. They can offer encouragement, support, and a different perspective, helping you to navigate through difficult times and emerge stronger.

Building strong social connections and cultivating a growth mindset are integral parts of developing inner strength. By nurturing relationships, seeking mentors, embracing challenges, and learning from failures, you lay a solid foundation for personal growth and resilience. Remember, the journey of self-improvement is ongoing, and every step you take is a step toward becoming a stronger, more adaptable, and resilient individual.

Practicing Self-Care

Self-care is an essential aspect of building and maintaining inner strength, especially during the teenage years when both body and mind are undergoing significant changes (Scott, 2020). It encompasses a broad spectrum of activities and practices that contribute to your overall well-being, enhancing your ability to cope with stress and challenges.

Prioritizing Mental Health

Mental health is just as important as physical health. It involves your emotional, psychological, and social well-being. How you think, feel, and act, how you handle stress, relate to others, and make choices—all these are part of your mental health (Plumptre, 2023).

Understanding and Managing Emotions

Recognize and accept your emotions as they come. Whether it's happiness, sadness, anger, or frustration, every feeling has a place in your life. Learning to manage these emotions is crucial. Techniques like journaling, meditation, or even talking to someone you trust can help you process your feelings effectively.

Stress Management Techniques

High school years can be stressful with academic pressures, social dynamics, and personal challenges. Developing stress management techniques is vital. Techniques such as deep breathing exercises, progressive muscle relaxation, and mindfulness can be easily incorporated into your daily routine and can significantly reduce stress levels (Rentala et al., 2019).

Seeking Help When Needed

There's no shame in seeking help when you're feeling overwhelmed. Talking to a counselor, therapist, or trusted adult can provide valuable support and guidance.

Maintaining Physical Health

Physical health plays a critical role in your overall well-being. A healthy body can significantly enhance your mental and emotional state.

Regular Exercise

Physical activity is known to improve mood, boost energy levels, and reduce symptoms of depression and anxiety. Find an activity you enjoy, whether it's a sport, dancing, yoga, or simply taking a walk. The key is consistency and making it a part of your daily routine.

Healthy Eating Habits

Nutrition has a direct impact on how you feel, think, and function. A balanced diet rich in fruits, vegetables, whole grains, and lean proteins can boost your mental and emotional well-being. Avoiding excessive junk food, sugary drinks, and caffeine can also help maintain a stable mood and energy level (Harvard School of Public Health, 2020).

Adequate Sleep

Teenagers need between 8–10 hours of sleep per night. Lack of sleep can affect your mood, energy levels, and ability to concentrate. Establish a regular sleep routine, limit screen time before bed, and create a comfortable sleeping environment to improve sleep quality (Suni & Dimitriu, 2023).

Expanding Your Knowledge and Skills

Expanding your knowledge and skills is about enhancing your abilities and gaining new insights. It's a lifelong journey that not only prepares you for the future but also enriches your personal life.

Continuous Learning

Continuous learning is the process of constantly expanding your knowledge and skills through various means. It's about being curious and open to new ideas, perspectives, and experiences.

Exploring Different Subjects

Don't limit your learning to school subjects. Explore areas outside your curriculum—art, music, literature, science, or any other field that interests you. This broadens your perspective and helps in developing a well-rounded personality.

Learning From Various Sources

In today's digital age, there are countless resources available for learning. Online courses, podcasts, documentaries, books, and educational apps offer endless opportunities to gain new knowledge. Take advantage of these resources to explore subjects you're interested in.

Practical Application

Applying what you learn in real-life situations reinforces your knowledge. Participate in science fairs, writing contests, or other activities that allow you to put your learning into practice.

Seeking New Experiences

Seeking new experiences is about stepping out of your comfort zone and trying things you've never done before. It enhances adaptability and resilience and broadens your understanding of the world.

Trying New Activities

Join clubs, sports teams, or other extracurricular activities. Trying new things can help you discover hidden talents and interests and also provide opportunities to meet new people and develop social skills.

Volunteering

Volunteering for a cause you care about can be a fulfilling experience. It not only contributes to personal growth but also provides a sense of accomplishment and empathy.

Traveling and Cultural Exposure

If possible, travel to new places. Experiencing different cultures broadens your horizons, increases tolerance, and provides a new perspective on life.

Creative Pursuits

Engaging in creative activities like writing, painting, or playing an instrument stimulates your mind, fosters creativity, and can be a great emotional outlet.

Developing Skill Sets

Developing skill sets involves both improving your existing skills and acquiring new ones. It's about understanding your potential and working toward enhancing it.

Personal Skills

Skills like time management, organization, and effective communication are essential in every aspect of life. Work on these skills through practice and by seeking feedback from peers, teachers, and mentors.

Professional Skills

Even as a teenager, you can start developing professional skills that will be useful in the future. Basic computer skills, public speaking, and writing are just a few examples. Look for workshops, online courses, or mentorship programs to develop these skills.

Technical Skills

In this digital age, technical skills are becoming increasingly important. Learning coding, graphic design, or how to use specific software can open up numerous opportunities in the future.

Managing Stress and Anxiety

In today's fast-paced world, stress and anxiety have become prevalent among teenagers (Divecha, 2019). Managing these effectively is crucial for maintaining both mental and physical health. Let's explore various strategies to handle stress and anxiety.

Understanding Stress and Anxiety

Stress is a response to an external cause, such as school deadlines or relationship issues, while anxiety is a reaction to stress. Recognizing the differences helps in addressing them appropriately.

Recognizing Stress Triggers

Identify what causes your stress. Is it academic pressure, social situations, or personal issues? Recognizing triggers is the first step in managing them.

Effective Time Management

Poor time management can lead to stress. Use planners or digital tools to organize your tasks. Prioritize your activities and set realistic goals.

Mindfulness and Meditation

Practices like mindfulness and meditation can significantly reduce stress levels. They involve focusing on the present moment and can help in calming your mind.

Physical Activity

Regular exercise is a powerful stress reliever. It might be a structured exercise program, a team sport, or just a daily walk. Physical activity produces endorphins, which are natural mood lifters.

Creative Outlets

Engaging in creative activities such as writing, painting, or playing a musical instrument can be therapeutic and help in managing stress and anxiety.

Building a Support System

Having a supportive group of friends or family members to talk to can make a huge difference. Sometimes, just talking about what you're going through can be a great way to unload some of the stress.

Healthy Eating Habits

What you eat can affect your mood and energy levels. A balanced diet can help in maintaining stable energy levels and improve overall well-being.

Sleep Hygiene

Lack of sleep significantly contributes to stress and anxiety. Establish a regular sleep schedule, create a restful environment, and avoid screens before bedtime to improve your sleep.

Seeking Professional Help

There are moments when stress and anxiety can become overpowering, and in such instances, it's perfectly acceptable to seek assistance from a counselor or psychologist. They can provide strategies and tools to manage your feelings more effectively.

Building Financial Responsibility

Financial responsibility is a crucial skill that is often overlooked in teenage years. Learning to manage your finances effectively can set you up for a lifetime of financial well-being.

The Basics of Budgeting

Learn the basics of creating and sticking to a budget. Track your income and expenses, and plan how you can save more and spend less.

Importance of Saving

Recognize the significance of setting aside funds for future requirements, such as emergencies. Begin with a modest savings target and progressively aim higher.

Smart Spending

Be a savvy spender. Learn to differentiate between wants and needs and make informed choices when spending money.

Using Financial Tools

Familiarize yourself with financial tools and apps that can help in tracking your spending and savings.

Part-Time Jobs

Consider taking a part-time job. It's not just about earning money; it's also about learning the value of hard work and responsibility.

Entrepreneurial Ventures

If you have a business idea, pursue it. It could be anything from tutoring to selling handmade crafts. This can teach you about entrepreneurship and financial management.

Savings Accounts

Open a savings account if you don't already have one. Learn about interest rates and how your money can grow over time.

Financial Education

Educate yourself about financial concepts. Read books, follow financial news, and even consider taking a class on personal finance.

Preparing for the Future

Preparing for the future is about setting yourself up for success in all areas of life. It involves career planning, developing life skills, and setting long-term goals.

Research Different Careers

Explore various career options. Look into fields that interest you and research the education and skills required for those careers.

Informational Interviews

Conduct informational interviews with professionals in fields you're interested in. This can provide valuable insights into what those jobs entail.

Internships and Volunteering

Gain practical experience through internships or volunteering. These opportunities provide a glimpse into different career paths and help build your resume.

Skill Development

Identify the skills required for your chosen career and work on developing them. This could be through formal education or self-learning.

Setting Long-Term Goals

Think about where you want to be in the next five or ten years. Set goals that are challenging yet achievable.

Action Plan

Create an action plan to achieve your long-term goals. Break down the plan into smaller steps and set deadlines for each step.

Adaptability

Be prepared to adapt your plans as needed. Life can be unpredictable, and flexibility is key to overcoming challenges.

Continuous Learning

Commit to lifelong learning. Keep updating your knowledge and skills to stay relevant in your chosen field.

Networking

Build a professional network. Connect with people in your field of interest, attend relevant events, and engage in online forums.

Unleashing Your Inner Strength

You've been on an incredible journey, diving deep into understanding your inner strength. It's a process that evolves continuously, and it's truly exciting to see how much you've grown and what you can still achieve. The journey of self-discovery is never-ending, and the more you learn about yourself, the more you can harness your unique strengths in everything you do. Let's explore how you can continue building on your strength with patience, understanding, and strategic thinking.

The Continuous Unfolding of Your Strength

You've made significant progress in connecting with your inner strength. It's important to recognize that this strength is not static; it evolves and grows as you do. Think of it like a tree, continually growing stronger and more resilient with each passing season. You've already seen changes in how you handle challenges and celebrate successes. This ongoing process is a testament to your ability to adapt and thrive.

Celebrate Your Progress

First off, give yourself a pat on the back. Recognizing and celebrating your growth is crucial. It reinforces your belief in your abilities and motivates you to keep pushing forward. Remember those moments when you felt strong and capable—they are your foundation for future growth.

Growth Through Challenges

Challenges are not just obstacles; they are opportunities for growth. Each time you face a difficult situation, you're tapping into and expanding your reservoir of strength. Reflect on recent challenges: How did you feel before, during, and after? What did you learn about your capabilities?

Patience in the Process

Building strength is not an overnight achievement. It requires time, patience, and persistence. The true extent of your strength is often revealed gradually.

The Power of Patience

Patience is essential, particularly in the realm of personal development. It's akin to tending a garden: You sow the seeds of strength, nourish them with experiences, and allow them the time they need to flourish. Be patient with yourself, especially during times when progress appears gradual.

Trust the Process

Even when you can't see immediate results, trust that the process is working. Just like roots grow beneath the surface before a plant emerges, your strength develops internally before it becomes apparent.

SWOT Analysis

A SWOT analysis (Strengths, Weaknesses, Opportunities, Threats) is an excellent tool for understanding yourself better. It can provide insights into how your strengths and weaknesses have shifted over time (Schooley, 2023).

Identifying Your Strengths and Weaknesses

Begin by listing your strengths and weaknesses. Be honest and objective. Strengths could include resilience, creativity, or empathy. Weaknesses might be impatience, fear of failure, or a tendency to procrastinate. Understanding these helps you to leverage your strengths more effectively and address your weaknesses.

Exploring Opportunities and Threats

Next, consider the opportunities and threats. Opportunities are external factors that you can take advantage of, like a new project or a mentorship program. Threats are external challenges you might face, such as peer pressure or a rapidly changing school environment.

Reflecting on Changes

Think about how your strengths and weaknesses have evolved since you started focusing on your inner growth. Perhaps a weakness has become less pronounced, or a strength has become more dominant. This reflection can guide your future growth strategies.

Applying Your Strength in Daily Life

Now, let's talk about integrating this newfound strength into your everyday actions.

Small Steps Lead to Big Changes

Start with small, manageable steps. Use your strengths in daily tasks, whether it's helping a friend, tackling homework, or engaging in a hobby. Each small victory builds your confidence and reinforces your growth.

Overcoming Obstacles

When faced with obstacles, remind yourself of your strengths. Approach challenges with the mindset that you have the tools and abilities to overcome them. This mindset shift can make a significant difference in how you handle difficulties.

Nurturing Your Strength for the Future

As you continue to grow, your understanding of your strength will also evolve. It's a lifelong journey.

Continuous Learning

Maintain a sense of curiosity and a willingness to learn. Immerse yourself in reading books, listening to podcasts, and participating in discussions that both challenge and inspire you. Continuous learning is a fundamental aspect of personal development.

Seeking Feedback and Support

Feel free to ask for feedback and support from friends, family, and mentors. Often, an external perspective can offer crucial insights into your strengths and areas where you can improve.

Embracing Change

Finally, embrace change. Your journey is unique, and your strengths will evolve as you navigate different experiences in life. Be open to this evolution and see where it takes you. Remember, building and understanding your inner strength is a continuous journey. It requires patience, reflection, and strategic thinking. Keep nurturing your strengths, addressing your weaknesses, and embracing opportunities for growth. Your journey is uniquely yours, and every step you take is a testament to your resilience and capacity for growth. Keep moving forward with confidence, knowing that your strength will shine through in all that you do. Keep growing, keep learning, and most importantly, keep believing in yourself.

Conclusion

As we draw the curtains on this book, let's take a moment to appreciate the journey you've embarked upon. This isn't just the conclusion of a book; it's a milestone in your ongoing journey of self-discovery and resilience. The insights and strategies outlined in these pages are tools for life, specially tailored for the dynamic and often unpredictable teenage years.

You've ventured through chapters that have not only introduced concepts but have also invited you to introspect and apply these lessons practically. From understanding the dynamic nature of your inner strength to embracing the power of patience, each section was crafted to guide you toward recognizing and harnessing your potential.

Importantly, this book is designed as a resource to be revisited. Each reading will unfold new meanings and insights, reflecting the changes and growth within you. The practice of revisiting and repetition is crucial. It helps in deeply internalizing the lessons learned, turning them from mere concepts into integral parts of your life's strategy.

Incorporating regular SWOT analyses into your routine is vital. This tool is not just a one-time exercise; it's a compass for continuous self-evaluation and development. By regularly assessing your Strengths, Weaknesses, Opportunities, and Threats, you'll gain a clearer understanding of your evolving self. This practice ensures that you're not just moving forward but also growing in the right direction.

Think of this book as a guide, a mentor that you can turn to when you feel lost, need inspiration, or simply want to check in with your progress. The chapters are designed to speak to you at different stages of your teenage years, offering wisdom that resonates with the challenges and triumphs you encounter.

As you step forward from here, remember that your journey of self-discovery is uniquely yours. It's filled with unique challenges but also unique strengths. Embrace every aspect of this journey, knowing that each experience is shaping you into a more resilient, insightful, and empowered individual.

Your inner strength is a living, evolving entity. It will grow, adapt, and become more nuanced as you navigate through life's experiences. Keep nurturing it with the lessons from this book, your personal experiences, and the wisdom you gather along the way.

In the end, remember that your journey of inner strength is never complete. It's a continuous path of learning, growing, and becoming. You have begun this journey with curiosity and courage, and these qualities will continue to guide you as you move forward.

Thank you for allowing this book to be a part of your remarkable journey. As you close this book, know that your journey of self-discovery and resilience is just beginning. Keep growing, keep learning, and always believe in the incredible power of your inner strength. The world is waiting to see the wonders you will achieve with it.

References

Ackerman, C. E. (2017, June 19). *Big five personality traits: The OCEAN model explained [2019 Upd.]*. PositivePsychology. https://positivepsychology.com/big-five-personality-theory/

Bromley, E., Johnson, J. G., & Cohen, P. (2006). Personality strengths in adolescence and decreased risk of developing mental health problems in early adulthood. *Comprehensive Psychiatry, 47*(4), 315–324. https://doi.org/10.1016/j.comppsych.2005.11.003

Cherry, K. (2013, November 29). *8 signs you're an introvert*. Verywell Mind.. https://www.verywellmind.com/signs-you-are-an-introvert-2795427

Cherry, K. (2023a, March 11). *What are the big 5 personality traits?* Verywell Mind. https://www.verywellmind.com/the-big-five-personality-dimensions-2795422

Cherry, K. (2023b, October 31). *An overview of the Myers-Briggs type indicator*. Verywell Mind. https://www.verywellmind.com/the-myers-briggs-type-indicator-2795583

Divecha, D. (2019, May 9). *Our teens are more stressed than ever: Why, and what can you do about it?* Developmental Science. https://www.developmentalscience.com/blog/2019/5/7/our-teens-are-more-stressed-than-ever

Gupta, S. (2023, May 26). *How self-reflection can improve your mental health*. Verywell Mind. https://www.verywellmind.com/self-reflection-importance-benefits-and-strategies-7500858

Harvard School of Public Health. (2020, May 1). *Nutrition and immunity*. The Nutrition Source. https://www.hsph.harvard.edu/nutritionsource/nutrition-and-immunity/

Johns, M. (2023, June 23). *Openness personality trait*. Thomas International. https://www.thomas.co/resources/type/hr-blog/openness-personality-trait#:~:text=Openness%20is%20how%20open%2Dminded

Kenton, W. (2023, October 30). *SWOT analysis: How to with table and example*. Investopedia. https://www.investopedia.com/terms/s/swot.asp

Leonardo, A. (2019, June 18). *The misconception of introvert (and extrovert)*. Medium. https://axelleonardo8.medium.com/the-misconception-of-introvert-and-extrovert-78a062be967e

Shapperd, A. (2023, October 6.). *Introvert communication tips to help prevent overwhelm*. Www.linkedin.com. Retrieved January 1, 2024, from https://www.linkedin.com/pulse/introvert-communication-tips-help-prevent-overwhelm-sam-sheppard-

National Institute of Mental Health. (2022). *Social anxiety disorder: More than just shyness*. https://www.nimh.nih.gov/health/publications/social-anxiety-disorder-more-than-just-shyness#:~:text=Social%20anxiety%20disorder%20is%20an

Newsom, R., & Rehman, A. (2020, December 4). *The connection between diet, exercise, and sleep*. Sleep Foundation. https://www.sleepfoundation.org/physical-health/diet-exercise-sleep

Oliver, J. (2023, October 10). *10 morning habits that will improve your health*. Medium. https://medium.com/@jordan.eng79/10-morning-habits-that-will-improve-your-health-2433790b988d

Plumptre, E. (2023, February 15). *The importance of mental health*. Verywell Mind. https://www.verywellmind.com/the-importance-of-mental-health-for-wellbeing-5207938

Reid, S. (2023, March 22). *Empathy*. Help Guide. https://www.helpguide.org/articles/relationships-communication/empathy.htm

Rentala, S., Thimmajja, S. G., Tilekar, S. D., Nayak, R. B., & Aladakatti, R. (2019). Impact of holistic stress management program on academic stress and well-being of Indian adolescent girls: A randomized controlled trial. *Journal of Education and Health Promotion*, 8. https://doi.org/10.4103/jehp.jehp_233_19

Schooley, S. (2023, September 1). *SWOT analysis: What it is and when to use it.* Business News Daily. https://www.businessnewsdaily.com/4245-swot-analysis.html

Scott, E. (2020). *5 self-care practices for every area of your life.* Verywell Mind. https://www.verywellmind.com/self-care-strategies-overall-stress-reduction-3144729

Segal, J., Smith, M., Robinson, L., & Shubin, J. (2023, February 28). *Improving emotional intelligence (EQ).* HelpGuide. https://www.helpguide.org/articles/mental-health/emotional-intelligence-eq.htm

Simkus, J. (2022, March 10). *Myers-Briggs type indicator: The 16 personality types.* Simply Psychology.org. https://www.simplypsychology.org/the-myers-briggs-type-indicator.html

Smith, J. (2020, September 25). *Growth mindset vs fixed mindset: how what you think affects what you achieve.* Mindset Health. https://www.mindsethealth.com/matter/growth-vs-fixed-mindset

Suni, E., & Dimitriu, A. (2023, October 4). *Sleep for teenagers.* Sleep Foundation. https://www.sleepfoundation.org/teens-and-sleep

The Myers-Briggs Company. (2009). *The history of the MBTI® assessment.* https://eu.themyersbriggs.com/en/tools/mbti/myers-briggs-history

Toussaint, L., Nguyen, Q. A., Roettger, C., Dixon, K., Offenbächer, M., Kohls, N., Hirsch, J., & Sirois, F. (2021). Effectiveness of progressive muscle relaxation, deep breathing, and guided imagery in promoting psychological and physiological states of relaxation. *Evidence-Based Complementary and Alternative Medicine*, *2021*(1), 1–8. https://doi.org/10.1155/2021/5924040

Widiger, T. A., & Oltmanns, J. R. (2017). Neuroticism is a fundamental domain of personality with enormous public health implications. *World Psychiatry*, *16*(2), 144–145. https://doi.org/10.1002/wps.20411

Zaman, B., & Jameel, R. (2021, March 18). *The fluid personality conundrum*. The Daily Star. https://www.thedailystar.net/shout/news/the-fluid-personality-conundrum-2062673

Made in the USA
Columbia, SC
16 September 2024

42431367R00067